Austria

AUSTRIA

by Frank Graham, JR.

WITH AN INTRODUCTION BY *Wilfried Platzer*

Austrian Ambassador to the United States

The Macmillan Company, New York
Collier-Macmillan Limited, London

To Jeannette Cogan, Mother and Teacher

Acknowledgments: Though this book is, in a very real sense, a labor of love, it could not have been finished without the contributions which others have made to it. The author wishes to thank Kurt Hampe of the Austrian Information Service in New York for his kindness in helping to assemble much of the material; Miss Sally Gates of Cambridge, Massachusetts, for her early encouragement; and Wilhelm Schlag of the Austrian Consulate in New York City, for his thoughtful reading and many helpful suggestions. The quotations on pages 8o and 96 from *The Handbook of Christian Feasts and Customs* by Francis Weiser are reprinted with the kind permission of Harcourt, Brace & World, Inc.

Picture credits: Austrian Information Service, pages viii, 10, 13, 14, 29, 30, 31, 33, 44, 45, 54, 70, 75, 78, 86, 91, 94, 98, 101, 102, 105, 108, 113, 115, 117 (bottom), 117 (top); Austrian Institute, pages 18, 85 (right), 89, 97; Austrian State Tourist Department, pages 4, 5, 19, 25, 35, 37, 38, 41, 43, 47, 49, 51, 53, 57, 58, 61, 62, 64, 68, 71, 72, 74, 75, 76, 82, 104, 107; Philip Gendreau, pages 3, 32; Rapho-Guillumette, frontispiece, pages 26, 85 (left); Wide World, pages 7, 23.

Contents

Introduction

BY WILFRIED PLATZER

AUSTRIAN AMBASSADOR TO THE UNITED STATES

Everybody knows Austrian music. The works of Mozart, Haydn, and Beethoven, the brilliant waltzes of Johann Strauss, and the best known of all Christmas carols, "Silent Night," are no longer the property of any one country—they are played and sung and loved all over the world. But they originated in a small country in the very heart of Europe—Austria.

We can thank Austria for more than music. More than once in past centuries that country saved our civilization, our way of life, from invaders from the East.

Austria is not a very rich country. It does not have the wealth of natural resources that has made other countries prosperous. But it has always had intelligent and hard-working people who never lost heart, no matter what happened to them. They have always kept their good humor and their warmhearted spirits, which have made them famous all over the world. These people know how to work, but they also know how to enjoy the good things in life. The Austrians like to be happy, as do all of us. And, although history has not given them too much reason for happiness, they always manage somehow to have a good time.

vi

Austria has a very long history. It goes back for more than four thousand years. Ruins have been found of settlements which existed in Austria more than two thousand years before the birth of Christ. When Columbus discovered the Americas, Austria was already a strong power in Central Europe, and it was to become even stronger. Much later, many people came from Austria to this country. They were courageous, energetic people, and their contributions are important to America to this day.

Because it was the center of the Austro-Hungarian Empire, and because of its location at the heart of Europe, Austria always attracted people from all parts of the continent. Slavs, Czechs, Hungarians, Poles, Germans, Italians, and Austrians, different as they are, have managed to live side by side for many centuries, even though at times they were not too friendly with each other. However, each of these peoples has contributed to the character of the country to make it truly European. Thus, Austria set an example of understanding and cooperation between peoples at a time when these things were not considered important.

A world that is split by a long and dangerous struggle needs such examples. Today, international understanding and cooperation are more important than ever. We must know each other and know more about each other, if we want to live together in peace and friendship. As the representative of Austria in the United States of America, I welcome you, therefore, to read this book, to find out for yourselves about my country, to find out about its beauty, its people, and its way of life.

A World of Treasures

❝Land of mountains, land of rivers,❞ begins the Austrian national anthem. When you look at Austria on the map and read its history, you will see why this tiny country of mountains and rivers is the "melting pot" of Europe.

Lying in the heart of Europe, Austria is neither in the north nor south, east nor west; or else it is in all of these. Its area is a little larger than the State of Maine, some 32,369 square miles. Its shape on a map resembles that of some odd little fish (swollen head and body with a wiggling tail, the city of Vienna its glittering eye). Within its borders stretch Western Europe's two greatest natural wonders—the Alps and the Danube River.

GREAT MOUNTAINS AND A GREAT RIVER

At first glance, the Alps are a tremendous obstacle to transportation of any kind. The most famous mountains in the world, they rise up before the astonished traveler as a mass of jagged rock, coated with snow and ice. They seem to form a steep wall, behind which an outnumbered people might defend themselves against an enemy, and which would discourage close relations with neighbors.

The grandest works of man are dwarfed by the size of the Alps. Lord Byron, the English poet, described a part of this strange world that rears up in the middle of Europe:

Mountains have fallen
Leaving a gap in the clouds, and with the shock
Rocking their Alpine brethren; filling up
The ripe green valleys with destruction's splinters;
Damming the rivers with a sudden dash,
Which crushed the waters into mist and made
Their fountains find another channel.

When you first see these splendid mountains, you may agree with the poet's explanation of their presence. They certainly seem to have fallen from the clouds, but a scientist's explanation is just as exciting. In the far-off past, before any human beings were here to see it, there was a great disturbance in the crust of the earth. Tremendous pressure pushed huge amounts of rock up from the south. Then the rock was broken, lifted up, and folded. Masses were thrust thousands of feet into the air.

This was the beginning of the Alps. The eastern part of this snow-covered barrier runs through Austria, fanning out into three chains. The central chain rises in granite peaks to heights of over eleven thousand feet. Running along its sides, on the north and south, are the two lower parallel mountain chains. Made of limestone rock, they were folded and eroded to form very steep slopes. Here the forests of evergreen trees thin out and finally disappear in the dry wind and sharp cold of the upper slopes; they are replaced by the weird shapes of rocky peaks.

Like the high waves of the ocean in a wild storm, the Alps are beautiful to see when one is among them, but one can easily come to harm in them. Their steep cliffs and deep gorges are traps for the unwary person who tries to climb or cross them. Parties of travelers and sportsmen have been overtaken by

A team of men and dogs rescues a victim of an Alpine snowslide.

sudden storms high in the mountains and have perished in the bitter cold and wind-driven snow.

Even the snow, so soft and delicate when it is falling, becomes a source of danger after it has reached the ground. Frequent blizzards may pile the snow too high on the steep slopes. Heavy masses of ice and snow weakly held are ready to tumble down the mountainside if they are knocked loose. Anything can set them off—a sudden gust of wind, the speeding edge of a ski, or even the vibrations from a loud call.

A great mass of loosened snow sliding down a mountain is called an avalanche. There are thousands of avalanches in the Alps every year. They carry with them any earth, rocks, and ice in their way. If trees, buildings, or people are caught in their path they too are picked up and swept along. Huge flurries of snow blot out the sun so that the snow itself looks black. A village that stands in the path of a large avalanche may be buried with all its inhabitants. Then only the tall steeple of the church stands uncovered, a tombstone for the village which lies buried there under thousands of tons of snow.

Yet parts of these mountains are more friendly to man and his work than this first glance might lead you to believe.

Usually thought of as the river of Vienna, the Danube is also the river of the Austrian countryside. Here it flows past quiet farms.

Glaciers—huge rivers of ice formed high in the mountains—help to cut and deepen the valleys. Over long periods of time the glaciers move slowly down the mountains, wearing away huge mounds of earth and rock, bit by bit. As the glaciers reach lower levels, portions of them melt and form streams. The streams grow into rivers, and the flowing waters help deepen the valleys. Valley openings, called passes, have thus been cut through the solid rock masses of mountain over the centuries.

The Danube River provides a trade route that offsets the barrier of the Alps. Western Europe's longest river, it rises in the Black Forest of Germany and finally empties, after a trip of over seventeen hundred miles, into the Black Sea. For 217 of those miles it runs within the territory of Austria. Since long before the time of Christ, the Danube has been a link between eastern and western Europe.

A way station rather than a barrier, Austria is thus located on one of the leading trade routes of Europe. Through the passes between the mountains, down the valleys scooped out by old glaciers and streams, and along the wide, choppy waters of the Danube, the traders of the ancient world brought precious goods from one side of the Alps to the other.

Amber and furs were carried from northern Europe over those Alpine passes to Rome. Cargoes of salt rock were rowed eastward along the Danube River in barges. Traders of all races were funneled into what is now Austria. Those same mountain passes and that same river remain important routes of communication today. But Austria has served as far more than a way station for the many peoples of Europe. When Vienna became the capital—first of the Holy Roman Empire and later of the Austro-Hungarian Empire—peoples with different backgrounds and different languages came together to serve one emperor.

A Vienna coffeehouse is a place to catch up on the news.

STRANGERS ARE NOT "STRANGE"

Austria, then, is a land where foreigners may feel at ease. Used to living alongside people whose manners and customs differ from theirs, the Austrians do not look on a stranger as someone who is "strange." They learned long ago the lessons of tolerance and compromise.

Austria has adopted many things from the people who passed through or settled down inside her borders. She has not been afraid to accept the ways of others, even of her enemies.

The habit of drinking coffee is an example. During the seventeenth century the Turks attacked Vienna. The terrible siege finally came to an end, and defeated Turks were forced to fall back. It is said that they left bags of coffee among their other abandoned belongings outside the walls of Vienna. Near starvation, the Viennese were unwilling to throw away anything. They prepared and tasted the strange drink, and liked it. Coffee became a standard Austrian drink. To this day, the coffeehouses of Vienna are famous all over the world.

At times this tolerance of other people has expanded into the most generous assistance. Seldom has a nation acted as splendidly as Austria did in 1956 when its neighbor, Hungary, revolted against the tyranny of Russia. Soviet tanks shot down the people in the streets and crushed the revolt. Thousands of panic-stricken Hungarians, having seen their country fall once more to the communists, rushed across the borders into Austria, Hungary's only free neighbor.

The Austrians were poorly prepared to offer any kind of assistance. They were just emerging from years of terror and hunger of their own. They could have done what many other nations have done when a flood of fleeing people appears to threaten their own well-being: close their borders. Instead, tiny Austria permitted over two hundred thousand Hungarians to cross the frontier.

It was a generous act, because it placed an additional burden on the Austrian people, who had already made many sacrifices. And it was a brave act because it displeased the communist powers, whose armies stood just beyond Austria's eastern frontier.

Americans, who have also accepted people from many lands, can understand and appreciate the Austrians. As you look at the people of Austria more closely, you will find some things about them that are familiar and some that are strange. Perhaps in the strangeness you will find here and there a custom or an attitude that will enrich your own lives. For Austria, a country of only 7,020,626 people (less than live in the city of New York), has a world of cultural treasures it is ready to share with the rest of mankind.

A group of Hungarians runs for the Austrian border—November 1956.

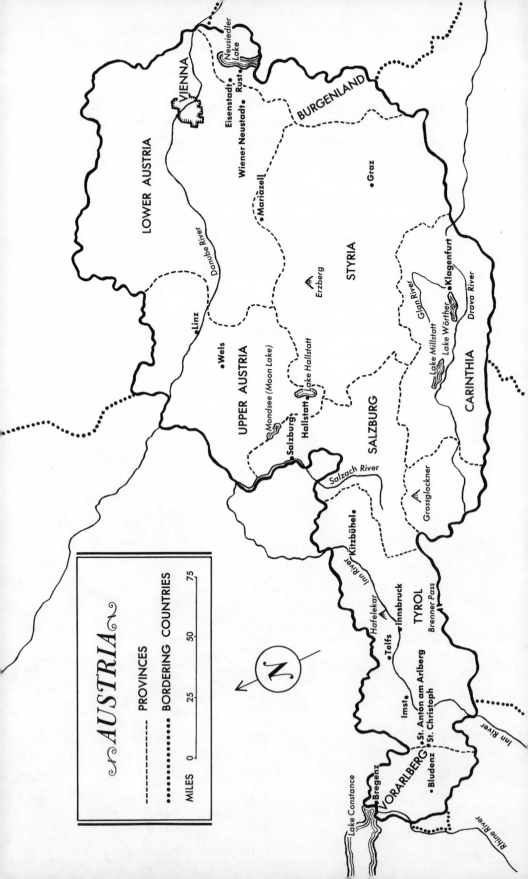

AUSTRIA

PROVINCES

·········· BORDERING COUNTRIES

MILES 0   25   50   75

N

VIENNA

Neusiedler Lake

Eisenstadt·
Rust·

BURGENLAND

Wiener Neustadt·

LOWER AUSTRIA

Graz·

Mariazell·

Danube River

STYRIA

Erzberg

Linz·

Glan River

Lake Millstatt

Lake Wörther

Klagenfurt·

Drava River

Wels·

UPPER AUSTRIA

Hallstatt· Lake Hallstatt

CARINTHIA

Mondsee (Moon Lake)

Salzburg·

SALZBURG

Salzach River

Grossglockner

Kitzbühel·

Inn River

Hafelekar

Telfs·

Innsbruck·

TYROL

Brenner Pass

Imst·

St. Anton am Arlberg

St. Christoph

Inn River

Bregenz·

VORARLBERG

Bludenz·

Lake Constance

Rhine River

2

The Beginnings

The land that is Austria today was "discovered" by the Romans shortly before the time of Christ. It already was inhabited, of course, just as America was inhabited when Columbus discovered it. But for a long time the lands north of the Alps had been largely unknown to the people who lived around the Mediterranean Sea.

Our Western civilization was born in that Mediterranean world. The nations to the north were considered savage, lands of perpetual mists and snow. There had been some contact with the north for centuries, however, since traders had first dared to cross the Alps. After the Romans had conquered all the lands around the Mediterranean, they began to look for other places where they could bring their civilization and where they could find new riches for their motherland.

The Romans wanted the iron mines which they knew existed in the mountainous regions now known as Styria and Carinthia. Pushing into what is now Austria (it had no such name then), the powerful Roman armies defeated the inhabitants and claimed the land as far north and east as the Danube River. The people who lived there were descended from two ancient groups: the Illyrians and the Celts.

No one knows exactly where the original home of the Celts was located, but they had come to central Europe from Asia

Ruins of the Roman city of Carnuntum, forty kilometers from Vienna

several hundred years before the Romans (about 400 B.C.). They were a pagan people who lived in walled villages. They had lively imaginations, and many of their gods and rituals still live on today as saints and feast days in Christianity.

After their defeat in A.D. 15, the Celts began to adopt the customs of Roman civilization. The Romans took over the Celtic settlement of Vindobona and made it a military base. Vindobona was to grow eventually into the beautiful city of Vienna. The countryside blossomed into fragrance and color as the Romans taught the Celts new methods of agriculture. Wheat, grapes, cherry trees, and peach trees were planted in the fertile soil. The land was now protected from the fierce barbarian tribes on the other side of the Danube.

Marcus Aurelius, the famous Roman emperor, took command of his armies on the Danube when they fought the barbarians. He made his headquarters at Vindobona for a time, and it was there that he died. Thinking of themselves now as Romans, the Celts abandoned paganism and accepted Christianity as it spread throughout the empire. For hundreds of years they lived fairly peacefully under Roman rule.

By the end of the fifth century, however, the mighty Roman Empire had crumbled. Barbarian tribes poured across the Danube River. Many people fled south to Rome. The ones who remained were ruled by a new race of invaders; the strongest of these Germanic tribes were the Bayuvarians. Sturdy, hard-working people, they can be called the first real Austrians.

Out of this movement of peoples back and forth a certain order began to appear. Most of the invaders were converted to Christianity, and soon churches and monasteries arose in the countryside. However, the occasional periods of peace during the next few centuries always ended in invasions and violence. Ever since the fall of the Roman Empire, there had been no single European state in continuous power.

THE BABENBERGS

Then a new idea spread throughout Europe. It was simply that all the different European states that were now Christian should be united into a new empire. The Pope was to be supreme in religious affairs, and an emperor was to be supreme in earthly affairs. A German was crowned the first emperor, and all the European states were supposed to accept his authority.

It didn't work out that way, of course. There were many quarrels and revolts. During the ninth century, the empire was invaded by the Magyars (Hungarians). A count named Leopold of Babenberg, who lived in a great castle overlooking the Danube, fought on the emperor's side against the invaders. When the Magyars were finally defeated in 955, Leopold was rewarded by being made the ruler of the lands on the eastern border of the empire. Even today the Austrians call their country *Österreich* (Eastern Kingdom), the name it was given in those days.

The Babenbergs, beginning in 976, ruled Austria for 270 years. From their strong castles they controlled the Danube. Later, they moved to Vienna, which had become an important city. It was again on one of the world's chief trade routes. People traveling to worship in the Holy Land passed through Austria. Later the Crusaders, Christian soldiers going to battle against the Mohammedans, also traveled through Austria.

Many of the Austrians, too, took part in the Crusades. One of the Babenbergs, Leopold V, led his soldiers in the fighting. After a while he neglected the war against the Mohammedans because of a bitter quarrel with a famous Christian warrior who had been fighting at his side. This warrior was Richard the Lionhearted, a king of England.

When Richard was on his way back to England in 1192, he made the mistake of passing through Austria. Leopold captured the handsome young English king and locked him up in the somber castle of Duernstein. A pretty story, known to almost every Austrian, is told about his rescue.

According to the legend, Richard's followers had no idea what had happened to him. Richard's loyal minstrel, Blondel, set out to find the king. Blondel wandered from castle to castle along the Danube. In front of each, it is said, he sang a song he had composed long before: "Oh, Richard, oh, my king."

He came at last to Duernstein, which was on one of the loveliest stretches of the river, about fifty miles from Vienna. There, against the hills where the apricot trees blossom in the spring and the vineyards stretch away as far as the eye can see, loomed the forbidding rough rocks of the castle walls.

Blondel once more began his plaintive song: "Oh, Richard, oh, my king."

Then, when he had finished the first stanza, there came from the castle an answering voice. It was King Richard, singing the second stanza in his gloomy cell. Overjoyed, Blondel hurried back to England with the news of Richard's whereabouts. The English asked the Austrians for his release and, after paying a huge sum of money in ransom, their king was returned to them.

The story of Blondel is only a legend, but the story of the ransom money is true. The German emperor, for whom Leopold had captured Richard, saw to it that the English quickly learned the fate of their king. When the ransom was paid, Leopold's share was used to fortify Austria's eastern borders.

It was a prosperous and colorful time for Austria. The court of Babenberg attracted many great poets and musicians. By the time the last of the Babenbergs was killed in battle in 1246, Austria had established itself as an independent country.

On the hilltop in the distance is the ruin of Duernstein Castle.

3

Empire to the Present

The land which had been ruled by the Baben-bergs for so many years now became a battlefield, as ambitious noblemen fought each other for the crown. Then, in 1273, Count Rudolf of Habsburg, the German king, won the struggle. The House of Habsburg kept the crown until, 645 years later, it was toppled in 1918. The Habsburgs were one of the most re-markable families in the history of the world.

By treaty and by marriage, but very seldom by war, the Habsburgs began to expand their territory. One by one the lands of Carinthia, Istria, and Vorarlberg were added to the Habsburg domain. It stretched far into the Alps in the west, into Hungary in the east, and to the Adriatic Sea in the south. In 1363, when the Alpine land of Tyrol joined Austria, the Habsburg ruler, Rudolf the Founder, boasted: "All roads and passes leading from Germany into Italy are subject to our rule."

In the western Alps, the Swiss were not happy under Austrian rule, and rose up in revolt to gain their independence. From that struggle has come the story of William Tell.

Though William Tell is a legendary character (like our Paul Bunyan) and the story has little truth, his image has remained an inspiration to liberty-loving people for hundreds of years. William Tell, the story goes, refused to obey Gessler, the

Austrian governor. Gessler arrested him and set a cruel punishment: Tell was ordered to shoot an apple off the head of his son. William Tell, however, did not hesitate. He picked up his bow and arrow, took aim at the apple, and shot it cleanly off his son's head. The boy was unharmed, but William Tell went back to prison, for he had sworn he would have killed the governor if the boy was hurt. Later he escaped, shot Gessler, and touched off the revolt that freed Switzerland.

By the fifteenth century Austria and the Habsburgs had won the respect of most of Europe. It was the custom then for the German-speaking countries to come together after the death of a Holy Roman Emperor and elect a new one. In 1438 a Habsburg was elected as Albert II. From that day until the Empire was dissolved in 1806, the title of Holy Roman Emperor remained almost continuously in the Habsburg family.

THE HOLY ROMAN EMPERORS

Strengthened by the title of emperor, the Habsburgs made a series of marriages that added greatly to their lands. In 1477, Maximilian of Austria married Mary, heiress to the crown of Burgundy, gaining most of what is now the Netherlands and Belgium. Their son Philip wed Johanna of Castile and Aragon, bringing Spain under the Habsburgs' rule. In 1515, Habsburgs married into the royal families of Hungary and Bohemia.

No wonder there was a motto in the Empire at the time that said: "Let others wage war; thou, happy Austria, marry."

A great part of the world was now governed under the "two-headed eagle," which was the emblem of the House of Habsburg. When Charles V, the greatest of the Habsburg emperors, came to the throne in the sixteenth century he ruled a domain on which "the sun never set." Including the Spanish territories which had just been discovered in the New World, Charles's empire stretched from Peru in South America to the Carpathian Mountains, east of the Danube Plain.

The Habsburgs were greatly involved in the important events of European history. Charles V fought for the unity of Christendom during the Reformation, backing the Pope against the Protestants: thus, Austria has been chiefly Roman Catholic to this day. The Emperor Ferdinand fought for control of the German states during the Thirty Years' War. Austria was one of the German states, in fact the most powerful of them, and German is still Austria's official language.

Perhaps an even greater responsibility for Austria, and for the Habsburgs as Holy Roman Emperors, was the defense of Europe against the Turks. Weakened by internal struggles, the European states had neglected the threat from the east. The Turkish sultans wanted to conquer Europe and make it a Mohammedan territory. For a while it appeared that the Turks would succeed. Their armies were more powerful than those of any western nation, and their navies were almost as strong. In 1571, they captured Cyprus and threatened to control the Mediterranean Sea. The Christian world was terrified to learn that the island's defenders had been slaughtered. The leader of the Cyprus garrison had been skinned alive and his skin, stuffed with straw, had been sent to the Turks' capital.

It was then that Don Juan of Austria (a Habsburg who had been born in Spain) was put in command of the European fleet and sent out to battle the Turks. He met the Turkish fleet near the Greek town of Lepanto in one of the greatest naval battles of modern times. Don Juan headed his flagship straight for the Turkish commander's. His troops swarmed aboard the enemy ship and captured it after a fierce hand-to-hand struggle. Panic spread through the rest of the Turkish fleet. Having been thoroughly beaten, the Turks turned and fled; of their powerful fleet, 117 ships were captured, 50 were sunk, and only 40 managed to escape. Don Juan's fleet had killed eight thousand Turks and captured ten thousand. Some twelve thousand Christians, who had been held as slaves by the Turks and forced to row their ships, were set free.

Despite this defeat at sea, the Turks, with their strong armies, remained a menace on land. Central Europe was constantly in danger, and Austria was the chief barrier against a Mohammedan attack. The French, who were bitter rivals of the Habsburgs for European leadership, encouraged the Turks to attack Austria and formed the so-called "Unholy Alliance" with them. In 1683, no country seemed strong enough to stop the Turkish army. It marched through eastern Europe and came right up to the walls of Vienna.

There the Austrians made a heroic stand. They refused to surrender the city. The Turks bombarded Vienna with their cannon and cut off the city's food supply. The bodies of the dead lay unburied in the streets. For two terrible months the defenders battled fire and starvation. At last help arrived. The Imperial German armies crossed the Danube, fired rockets to tell the people of Vienna that they were saved, and rushed at the Turkish army. The Turks fell back. A final counterattack by the Turkish cavalry failed, and the battle was over. The Turks fled back toward Hungary, leaving their treasure (and those bags of coffee) behind. They never seriously threatened Europe again.

Detail of the old Vienna walls that held back the Turks in 1683

The two-headed Habsburg eagle on the roof of St. Stephen's Cathedral

THE HABSBURG GOVERNMENT

Voltaire, the great French writer, once said that the "Holy Roman Empire was neither holy, Roman, nor an empire." He was right, of course. It was, however, successful in bringing some order out of the confusion that reigned in Europe for so many years. During the eighteenth century the Empire survived through many bitter European wars, but its power and influence gradually weakened.

It will be worth our while to look closely for a moment at the composition of the Habsburg government. Austria, naturally, was its heart. The larger territory, known as the Holy Roman Empire, was composed of a number of countries which were mostly German-speaking. These had their own rulers who recognized the Habsburgs as the leaders of their loose association.

This association helped to make Vienna a world capital. Austria, and the Empire, too, at times, were ruled from Vienna, where a complicated system of government had been set up. The big decisions were made by the emperor. However, after the sixteenth century he had little actual political power, since he did not take part in the internal government of his subject lands. Most of the ordinary matters of government were handled by a hard-working and loyal civil service, called *Der Allerhoechste Dienst* (the Most High Service).

The people were content to be ruled by these "experts." For that reason the Austrians did not become accustomed to governing themselves, and democracy developed there later than it did in some other parts of Europe.

Men from all over Europe served under the emperor. Many of the names of the emperor's military commanders sound Italian, Spanish, or Hungarian, rather than Austrian. Don Juan, the Austrian admiral who commanded the Christian fleet at Lepanto, had a Spanish name. Raimund Montecuccoli, who led the emperor's troops against the Turks, had an Italian name. It was said that it was impossible to be a foreigner in Vienna.

Austria itself had this international character. It was made up of a number of *laender*, individual territories such as Tyrol, Vorarlberg, Bohemia, and Carinthia, much like the states which compose the United States. Though the *laender* had a measure of independence within the Austrian government and even spoke languages other than German, the emperor was supreme.

Disaster struck this great empire at the beginning of the nineteenth century. The Habsburgs came into conflict with the young Corsican soldier who had become emperor of France—Napoleon Bonaparte. The greatest military genius in modern history, he seemed for a long while to be unbeatable. He defeated the Russo-Austrian army at Austerlitz in 1805, and the Habsburg emperor was forced to make peace. Control of the German states was now in French hands. Francis II, the last Holy Roman Emperor, gave up the imperial title the following year. The Habsburgs still clung to their rule in Austria, but they moved in the shadow of the great French ruler. In 1809 Andreas Hofer lead the Tyrolean peasants in an unsuccessful revolt against Napoleon. The peasants were defeated, and Hofer died a hero's death.

Klemens Metternich, who became Austria's foreign minister in that year, was one of the cleverest statesmen Europe has ever had. He made every possible move to keep Austria from being crushed. He pretended to join Napoleon's side. He arranged for the Habsburg princess, Marie Louise, to marry Napoleon. This was ironic, for the French revolutionaries had beheaded Marie Louise's great-aunt, Marie Antoinette.

Metternich's policy of waiting was finally rewarded. Napoleon's army was weakened by the hardships of fighting during a Russian winter. In 1813, the allied troops under Austrian Prince Schwarzenberg nearly destroyed the French army at Leipzig. This important battle led to Napoleon's final defeat.

Europe, shattered by war, now tried to pick up the pieces. Metternich, in the name of the Austrian emperor, played a leading part in planning Europe's recovery. The rulers of all the great nations met at the Congress of Vienna, where, against a background of gaiety, a program was planned to keep order in Europe. The peace lasted for about a hundred years.

Austria, though it no longer controlled the territory it once had under the Holy Roman Empire in northern and western Europe, was still one of the most powerful countries in the world. It was made up of many peoples: Germans, Hungarians, Czechs and Slovaks, Poles, Ruthenians, Serbs and Croats,

Romanians, Slovenes, and Italians. When, in the middle of the nineteenth century, the Hungarians became especially strong, they were given more independence, and the dual country came to be called the Austro-Hungarian Empire.

The Habsburgs still continued to cling to their power. The Austro-Hungarian Empire was able to produce most of the food and goods it needed, and so survived in the changing world. But there were many signs of weakness. Quarrels broke out among the various peoples within the Empire. Outside it, Prussia was rising to rival Austria for the leadership of the German-speaking world.

INTO THE TWENTIETH CENTURY

In 1866, Prussia and Italy attacked Austria. The Habsburgs lost part of their territory to Italy, and Austria was put out of the German Confederation. Bismarck, the Prussian leader, summed up the Austrian defeat when he said: "The German question was settled by blood and iron."

When the twentieth century began, the Austro-Hungarian Empire still commanded a certain amount of respect, but it had lost its strength, and could not survive World War I, which began when the heir to the Habsburg crown was assassinated. When Austro-Hungary turned out to be on the losing side, the last of the Habsburg emperors was forced to give up his throne, and the Empire was dissolved. The various peoples that had been a part of the empire now joined other countries or formed new nations of their own: Czechoslovakia, Yugoslavia, Hungary. It was then that Austria became a republic and shrank into the little nation you see on the map today.

There was only misfortune ahead for Austria. The harsh treaty it had been forced to sign at the end of World War I kept it from making a comeback. Many people went without jobs, and some starved. Unrest spread through Vienna, a giant capital with too small a country. Then came a man who was to bring Austria even more grief.

Adolf Hitler was born in 1889 in the little Austrian town of Brannau, near the German border. As a young man he went to Vienna, where he hoped to become a painter, but his work was turned down by the Vienna art schools. Angry and disappointed, he left Austria to settle in Germany. There he began his remarkable and savage political career.

Once a fashionable shopping street, Kärtnerstrasse in 1945 shows the heavy damage inflicted on Vienna by World War II bombings.

As dictator of Germany, Hitler was determined to bring all the German-speaking people of Europe under his rule. There were some Austrians who believed that their country could solve its problems by joining itself to Germany. Hitler's armies marched into Austria in 1938 and took over.

Hitler imposed the Nazi dictatorship on the unfortunate Austrians and when World War II broke out in 1939, they fought on the German side. Their cities were heavily bombed. At the end of the war they once more faced starvation, as well as the task of rebuilding their shattered cities. Vienna itself was severely damaged. St. Stephen's Cathedral had burned; the beloved Opera House was in ruins.

THE AUSTRIANS REBUILD

The Austrian people did not become discouraged through all these hardships. They scraped together what they could to eat, and they used their last pennies to attend the theater, which had been for so long a part of their way of life. With the aid of America's Marshall Plan, they recovered more quickly than they had after World War I.

Slowly Vienna arose again from the ruins. The Opera House was rebuilt. On April 26, 1952, the new *Pummerin*, a bell for St. Stephen's, was carried in triumph through the city's streets, and the people cheered as it was taken into the cathedral. Long a symbol as dear to the Austrians as the Liberty Bell is to Americans, the original *Pummerin* had been made from Turkish guns captured after the siege of Vienna in 1683.

On May 15, 1955, Austria regained its freedom. A State Treaty was signed with the Allied nations in Vienna, and the armies of the United States, Great Britain, France, and the Soviet Union, which had occupied Austria since the end of World War II, marched away. The Austrians were once again masters of their own country.

The new Pummerin *on its way to St. Stephen's Cathedral in 1952*

4

Vienna

Unless you knew tiny Austria's history, you would be astonished by the size and brilliance of her capital city. Of the country's seven million inhabitants, more than one and one-half million live in Vienna. Along its famous streets are some of the most beautiful buildings in the world. Its museums house numberless treasures of art. The music, the wonders of science, and all the other good things which its people have created, now profit and gladden the rest of mankind.

Vienna is a product of the vast Empire it once ruled. It is hard to forget that the flourishing Roman outpost of Vindobona used to stand on this site, and that an important trading town, Vienna, replaced it in the Middle Ages. As the heart of the Habsburg domain, Vienna was lively and gay for over six hundred years. Everywhere you look in Vienna today, you see that special blend of races and cultures that has made it a city of such great variety.

Though the city's glory is built on the industry of its citizens, it is the charm, the gaiety, and the grandeur that the visitor is likely to see. Few of the world's big capitals lie in so lovely a setting. Vienna is in the far eastern part of Austria. Just beyond the city rise the sunny slopes where, almost two thousand years ago, the Romans planted the vineyards which produced the first fine Austrian wines. Today row after row of grapevines still cover the hills.

On three sides of the city lie the Vienna Woods. These country surroundings still hold the charm they had over a century ago when Beethoven, one of the greatest composers who ever lived, used to walk to them from his Vienna home.

"Here in this countryside I often sit for hours," Beethoven once wrote, "feasting my senses. No one could love this countryside more than I do."

Part of Vienna's strength comes from the mighty Danube River on which boatmen for centuries have brought in food and products from other areas. The Danube itself does not actually flow through the city. The waterway we see in Vienna is the Danube Canal, which branches off from the river to run a short distance along the edge of the Inner City. And the river is not the "Blue Danube" we hear about in the song. The Danube near Vienna is murky because of the soil carried in it from the mountains. But its dark waters do not mar the city's charm. Neither do the bleak days of winter, when the chill gray sky snuffs out the sun and the street lights sometimes glow all day long.

When you visit Vienna, you will probably go first to the Inner City. This is the section that used to be surrounded by the stout walls which protected the city. During the nineteenth century the walls were torn down. In their place today a broad boulevard runs in a giant U-shaped course from the Danube Canal, around the Inner City, and back again at last to the Canal. It is called the *Ringstrasse* (Ring Street).

VIENNA'S BUILDINGS

Along the *Ringstrasse* you can see some of Vienna's most impressive buildings: the Opera House, the *Burgtheater* (National Theater), the Museum of Natural History, the Museum

At Klosterneuberg, one of the many vineyards just outside Vienna

of Art History, the University of Vienna, the City Hall, the Parliament Building, and the *Hofburg* (Court Castle), used by the rulers of Austria from the time of the Babenbergs.

Most of Vienna's old buildings, however, are not museums. It is a living city, and people live and work in the palaces which are monuments to past ages. The President of Austria has his offices in the *Hofburg*. In other palaces you will find government offices, foreign embassies, or the residences of high officials.

At the center of the Inner City is the majestic St. Stephen's Cathedral. Its spire, reaching four hundred feet above the streets, dominates the city. In past centuries the spire was used as a watchtower to search the surrounding countryside for enemy armies. It was also used until very recently as a fire tower from which watchmen kept an eye on the city and immediately sounded the alarm if a fire was seen. On a part of the cathedral's sloping roof, colored tiles form a picture of the Habsburg's two-headed eagle.

Along the streets of the Inner City are very attractive shops, displaying food and wares which are hard to ignore. There are stores stocked with the latest clothes, for Vienna is one of Europe's fashion centers. There are windows crammed with enormous sausages and gaily wrapped cheeses and dark-toned smoked fish, for nowhere will you find better delicatessens than in Vienna.

The shops which sell candies and cakes are famous all over the world. If you are lucky enough to be in Vienna at Christmastime you will see all manner of outlandish and tasty creatures in the shop windows: saints of marzipan (a candy

made of crushed almonds, sugar, and egg whites), angels of sparkling sugar, and Krampus, who comes with St. Nicholas, made of chocolate with a long scarlet tongue and a slender rod of gold in his hand.

Almost anywhere you look in Vienna you will find a coffeehouse. These are warm, comfortable places, very different from the little "eateries" in the United States where one drops in only for a few minutes to gulp down a coffee and doughnut and then hurries away. In Vienna the coffeehouse is designed for leisure. If a person orders a cup of coffee (he has many varieties to choose from) he is entitled to keep his table as long as he likes. He can meet his friends there, or play chess, or read his favorite newspaper. On racks near the wall he will find all the local newspapers, and even some foreign ones, stretched on bamboo poles.

LEFT: *The Burgtheater on Ringstrasse. The spire of St. Stephen's is seen in the distance.* RIGHT: *People, as well as buildings, contribute to Vienna's charm. This man rests his horses in front of the Opera House.*

You can buy pastries in the Prater without leaving your sunny bench.

VIENNA PRATER

There is much to see in Vienna outside the Inner City. Stretching for almost four miles between the Danube Canal and the Danube River is a large park called the Prater. You will be able to find your way to the park from any part of Vienna because its enormous Ferris wheel can be seen for miles around. Long ago, the Prater was the place where wealthy people hunted. Then the Emperor Joseph, a wise ruler who was known as "The People's Friend," decided that all the people of the city could go there. The mighty lords and ladies were very angry. They said that the Prater should be a place where they could mingle with their equals.

The Emperor had a sharp reply to these snobbish nobles who were always scheming to be in his company. "If I wanted to be only with *my* equals," he told them, "I would have to spend all my time in the Capuchin Church where the Habsburgs are buried."

Today the Prater is a delightful place for everybody, the young and the old, the rich and the poor. There is the Ferris wheel and many other carnival rides, race tracks, restaurants, coffeehouses, and a fine sports stadium. And there is the marvelous Punch-and-Judy show for which the Prater is famous. Most important of all, perhaps, for the city dwellers, is the Prater's great expanse of fields and woods, where one can wander under the old chestnut trees or lie for a while in the grass, reading or dreaming.

VIENNA'S SPECIAL ATTRACTIONS

Some of Vienna's greatest palaces stand outside the Inner City. There is the Belvedere Palace, where the State Treaty which gave Austria back its independence was signed in 1955.

An elaborately decorated Imperial coach in the Carriage Museum

This palace was built more than two hundred and fifty years ago by Eugene of Savoy. Eugene was a young French nobleman who had been kept out of the army by his king because he was thought to be "too puny" for military life. Like so many other talented people of his time, Eugene entered the service of the Habsburg emperor. Eugene commanded a regiment of the Imperial army to defeat the Turks and raise the siege of Vienna in 1683. He went on to become one of the finest soldiers in European history. Settling in Vienna, he built his magnificent Belvedere Palace. Belvedere means "beautiful view," and that is what this palace has: a beautiful view out over Vienna to the hills and woods beyond.

Another palace which is well named is the Schönbrunn, which means "beautiful fountains." Set among lovely gardens and fountains, this palace is one of the most impressive in Europe. Many of the Habsburgs lived there, including Maria Theresa, the eighteenth century empress who was among the wisest of all the Habsburg rulers. Napoleon also lived there for a time.

Inside, the Schönbrunn is luxurious. You walk through a seemingly endless series of rooms decorated with huge mirrors, bronze chandeliers, and rich paintings of long-dead Habsburgs. You will see the little Schönbrunn Theater, gaily decorated in red, white, and gold. There Mozart conducted one of his own operas, and there, too, the beautiful Habsburg princess, Marie Antoinette, acted the part of a shepherdess in little palace plays. This was the same Marie Antoinette who later married the king of France and died on the guillotine during the French Revolution.

Another place to visit is the Carriage Museum, whose prize exhibit is a carriage shaped like an enormous golden crown. Pulled by eight magnificent horses, the emperor used to ride in this carriage to his coronation. Until you see it, you will hardly believe that anything like it existed outside a fairy tale.

The Lippizaner horses perform under ornate crystal chandeliers.

Vienna, of course, has more than famous buildings to offer its visitors. The Vienna Choir Boys were organized by the Emperor Maximilian in 1489. The city is searched continually for young boys with fine singing voices. The lucky ones who are chosen for the Choir are given expert musical training. But you do not have to go to Austria to be entertained by them. They have become so famous that they are in demand all over the world. One of their groups is always traveling, while the rest remain in Vienna to give concerts or to sing at Mass in the Hofburg Chapel. From this choir have come many of Austria's finest musicians, including the composer Franz Schubert. Both Mozart and Haydn composed music for the Vienna Choir Boys.

An old Vienna institution is the Spanish Riding School. Its stately building is the home of the world-famous Lippizaner Horses. These beautiful snow-white stallions are trained to go through the most difficult movements and routines without a mistake. They took part in the first television broadcast from Europe to the United States using the Telstar communications satellite.

Toward the end of World War II, Vienna was being bombed, and the horses were moved to Bohemia (Czechoslovakia). When the Russians occupied that country, the Viennese were afraid that their valuable horses would be taken away from them. The commander of the Spanish Riding School asked America's General George Patton to help preserve this part of Austria's national heritage. General Patton agreed, and arranged to have the horses moved to the town of Wels, which was then controlled by the United States Army. The horses were thus saved for Vienna, and today you can see them there—performing with a combination of beauty and precision seldom reached by any other group of animals.

VIENNA'S INDUSTRIES

Beneath all the charm and glitter you will find that the Viennese people work as hard as anyone else. Vienna is Austria's industrial center, as well as one of the world's entertainment centers. Here are located factories producing clothing, food, furniture, chemicals, leather goods, and medical supplies.

The artistic nature of the Viennese worker is even revealed in the wares he produces. Vienna porcelain has been among

The Barbara Pipeline Bridge carries natural gas for industrial use across the Danube at Mannswoerth, near Vienna.

the world's best since 1717, when a Dutchman named Du Paquier founded a factory there. Today sparkling dishes and cups and jugs, decorated with charming little figures and flowers, continue to flow into homes where fine objects are treasured. The products of the Augarten Porcelain factory are masterpieces of their kind. And from earliest times the Viennese have designed and made fine jewelry.

Despite the sadness that has fallen on Vienna so often in her long and stormy history, the hard-working citizens are still creating things—as grand as a palace or as delicate as a teacup—that bring pleasure to people throughout the world.

5

Tyrol

When most of us picture Austria to ourselves, it is Tyrol that comes to mind, just as a young Austrian is likely to imagine the United States as one vast Wild West. Tyrol is the land of craggy high mountains, of snug farmhouses dotting the lower slopes, of dashing skiers, and of ruddy-faced yodelers in short leather pants. Here is a province where you will be charmed by the shapes, colors, and sounds that man has made, and you will always be aware of nature's majesty.

Tyrol has been a province for almost a thousand years. It came into being as an independent land, ruled by the counts of Tyrol, and then joined Austria in 1363. After World War I, the southern part of Tyrol was taken from Austria by Italy, and the two remaining parts, Tyrol and East Tyrol, are separated now by a narrow strip of the Salzburg Lande. Though Tyrol is one of the nine provinces, or *laender,* that make up Austria, it has a great deal of freedom to govern itself.

THE MOUNTAINS

Most of the people of Tyrol live in the valleys or on the lower slopes of the mountains, but it is the mountains themselves that give the province its special character. They rise to dizzying heights, cutting off one village from another. Travel between two villages is often possible only by way of roundabout valley roads or over high passes between the peaks.

A famous mountain climber, asked why he risked his life to climb an Alpine peak, replied: "Because it is there." You will know what he meant when you see those lofty mountains. Even if you do not try to climb the highest peaks, you will want to explore their lower approaches, for the mountain world, like the world of the sea or the desert, is a fascinating place.

In spring the mountain slopes are spattered with color; the wild flowers are in bloom. As you start up you will find columbine and lilies-of-the-valley and, here and there, rhododendron and blueberry shrubs. Perhaps an Apollo butterfly, its wings spotted with bright red, will flutter for a moment and then go off, dipping and soaring among the flowers.

After the blooms of spring flowers in May and June have disappeared, there will be more for you to see. There will be forests of birch and larch trees, meadows of grasses and legumes, and fields of crops. In autumn the needles of the larch turn yellow and fall to carpet the ground. Higher still, where the forests thin out, the stone pines grow straight and tall, as if they are proud to have withstood so many bitter storms at that level. If you manage to climb this high, you will see the forests come to an end in the twisted, stunted shapes of larches and fir trees which bear marks of their struggle with the cold and the wind.

As the forests disappear, sometimes there are smooth green carpets of grass. In these Alpine meadows cattle and other livestock graze in summer. As you breathe deeply and look around at the peaks, you will find that a few flowers do grow. Buttercups and forget-me-nots, crocuses and blue gentians brighten the bleak wasteland with color.

Highest of all, growing among rocks where traces of snow may still linger, is the little edelweiss. This tiny white flower is a symbol of purity, and its name, "edel-weiss," means "noble white" in German. In the Alps, there are many stories of people who have been killed trying to pick the lovely edelweiss on jagged, slippery peaks.

Small Tyrolean villages show few signs of the twentieth century.

In winter, curiously enough, it can be warmer on the mountains than in the valleys. The heavier cold air drops into the valleys, and often layers of cloud form just above. The sun shines hotly through the clear air on the snow-covered upper slopes, but its rays do not pass through the cloud covering to warm the valleys below.

An even more curious feature of Alpine weather is the *foehn* (pronounced FERN), a hot, dry wind which appears suddenly out of the south and lasts for several days at a time. When it blows, the air warms quickly. The heavy air of the *foehn* carries electrical charges with it. This jangles people's nerves, and, when things go wrong, they shake their heads and complain to each other: "It's the wind, the wind." On days when the *foehn* blows, people may be so upset that they will cancel business or social appointments and simply stay at home. These warming, drying winds sometimes melt off the snow, and livestock can then graze and children can play.

MOUNTAIN VILLAGES

In the valleys of Tyrol and here and there on the lower slopes are the little villages that have charmed visitors for centuries. Grouped around the church, the buildings are neat and clean. Some of them have gay or sacred scenes painted on their outside walls; nearly all of them have vines on the walls and flowers at the windows.

In the village square there usually stands a fountain, perhaps decorated with the statue of a saint. The women come here to draw water, and the cattle come to drink from a large tub next to the fountain. Nearby might be found the little wine-house where the men gather after work and on Sundays.

Stretching out from the village along the valley or spreading up the slopes above it are clusters of farmhouses. The typical farmhouse is a two- or three-story building with a lower level of whitewashed stone and an upper part of dark, unpainted wood. Its gently sloping roof extends well beyond the walls to protect the house from rain and snow. On the roof are a number of heavy stones to keep it from being lifted up and carried away during one of Tyrol's fierce storms.

Attached to the second story, and facing south to catch the rays of the sun, there may be a long balcony. Here the house-wife grows bright red geraniums on the railings in summer. In winter, the balcony may be used as a place to hang the family wash.

The wood-paneled rooms downstairs are heated by a huge porcelain stove, often painted with little scenes of rural life. Double windows, and walls sometimes twenty inches thick, help to keep out the cold and retain the heat. There is generally no heat in the rooms upstairs. On cold nights in winter the people quickly get out of their clothes and, shivering, climb into their beds, snug under the big pillow-like covers that create as much warmth as our heavy quilts.

Many of the people in Tyrol cling to their old customs, and, whenever there is the slightest excuse, they dress up in clothes like those their ancestors wore. A religious feast day or a national holiday, even a wedding or a first communion, brings the people into the streets in their lovely old-fashioned clothes.

On such occasions the women wear long, full skirts, blouses with billowing sleeves, black scarves around the shoulders and tucked in at the waist, aprons of various colors and

Behind these two Tyrolean villagers in traditional costumes, you can see a typical house with painted decorations and long balcony.

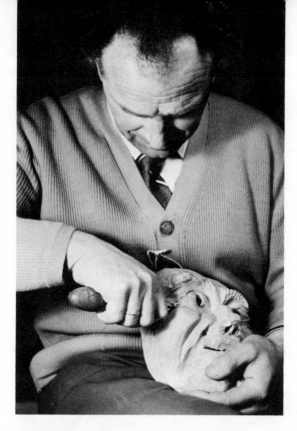

*A wood carver at work on one of over 500 masks
for the* Schemenlaufen

intricate designs, large kerchiefs and handsome hats, and low-buckled shoes. The *dirndl* dress, which has been copied in America, is always worn in Tyrol with an apron.

The men at these celebrations dress just as colorfully: broad-brimmed hats, black kerchiefs, woolen jackets, colorfully embroidered suspenders, knee breeches of wool or leather, and knee-length white woolen stockings. At other times the men wear short leather pants and narrow-brimmed "Tyrolean" hats, set off with a decoration that looks like a shaving brush. This decoration is a *gamsbart,* which means "beard of the chamois." It is really made of the hairs plucked from the back of the chamois, an agile, goatlike antelope of the higher Alps, and gathered into a cluster in a silver holder.

Most of the people in the mountain villages make their living from farming or, perhaps, from running little shops or wine-

A mummer teases the spectators during the Schemenlaufen *parade, which has been held in Imst every fifth year for many centuries.*

houses which mainly serve the villagers. These people do not earn very much money, and their villages change little from year to year. But some Tyrolean towns have grown prosperous because they are popular with tourists and sportsmen.

The villages of Imst and Telfs, for instance, stage traditional spring festivals in which the people dress up in their costumes or put on horrible masks and wind through the streets in colorful processions. Villages in valleys like Ziller attract mountain climbers, who come to scale the rugged peaks above it. Other villages are crowded during the summer because of their cool, clear mountain lakes.

Most prosperous of all the recreation towns are those which have good skiing conditions nearby. Skiing has become an important source of income undreamed of fifty years ago. The Arlberg region of western Tyrol has many steep snow-covered mountains. The modern school of Alpine skiing was developed here. St. Anton am Arlberg is one of the world's most famous ski centers. Just above it lies St. Christopher, another ski center on the road to the Arlberg Pass.

Farther east in Tyrol is Kitzbühel. Only seven thousand people live there, but the town entertains over sixty thousand visitors every year. When the snow lies on the sunny slopes above the town, Kitzbühel prepares to receive swarms of people who journey there from all over Europe to ski. Then its inns, restaurants, souvenir shops, and sporting goods stores do a flourishing business.

INNSBRUCK

Like the Viennese, the Tyrolese are used to foreign faces. Tyrol lies on one of Europe's principal travel routes, between Germany on the north and Italy on the south. For thousands of years travelers and traders have crossed the Alps by way of Tyrol, entering it through the northern passes and heading south toward Italy through the most famous of all Alpine gateways, the 4,500-foot-high Brenner Pass.

An important town was certain to grow up on this much-traveled route. It was founded on the banks of the Inn, a broad river flowing through the center of Tyrol. Thus the town came to be called Innsbruck, which is German for "Inn's bridge." The discovery of ancient stone and bronze tools around Innsbruck proves that settlements have existed thereabouts for more than three thousand years.

A first glimpse of Innsbruck is especially exciting if you come to it from the south. After leaving Italy through the Brenner Pass, you drive for twenty-five miles along a modern mountain road that winds through rich green forests. Suddenly, around a bend in the road, lying in the broad Inn Valley below, with the bold limestone mountains of the North Range rising abruptly above it on the other side, is the city of Innsbruck.

Stadium for the 1964 Olympic Games under construction in Innsbruck

The poet Rudolph Baumbach, probably with this view in mind, has called it "a flashing pearl in laurel wreaths."

Tourists crowd into Innsbruck and the surrounding resorts each winter to ski on the steep mountains. Its excellent ski trails and facilities won for Innsbruck the honor of playing host to the 1964 Olympic Games. Those challenging ski trails also bring many people to grief, and the streets of Innsbruck resound to the thump of leg casts against pavements as the broken-legged skiers limp about as best they can.

Innsbruck is now a modern city of over a hundred thousand people. It is a railroad hub of considerable importance and a rapidly growing industrial center. The buildings long ago spread over both banks of the Inn, and now its new structures climb the slopes of the mountains to the north and south. Its university, founded in 1677, attracts many students from America.

Everywhere in this modern city you can find reminders of the past. There is the imposing *Hofburg,* where some of the Habsburgs lived, including Emperor Maximilian I, who liked to call Tyrol "the heart and shield of the empire." In turn, the Tyrolese called him "Emperor Max" (but not to his face). Nearby, in the Court Church, the magnificent tomb shown here was built for him. It includes twenty-eight enormous bronze statues of famous rulers and warriors of the Middle Ages. These "Iron Men" were supposed to guard the body of their peer, Maximilian, but they guard only an empty tomb, because Maximilian is buried in eastern Austria.

Nearby, the Court Garden, where royalty once walked, is now open to the public. Many of its lovely old trees were destroyed by bombs in World War II, but new trees have been set out. In spring the gardeners plant all sorts of flowers which bring the beds, bordering the shady, twisting walks, alive in a burst of color. There you can see the funny little squirrels with long, pointed ears, like rabbits. Tiny, blue-capped birds, which are something like American chickadees, flit down from the low-hanging branches to snatch bread crumbs from your hands.

The city's main street is the Maria Theresienstrasse, named for the Habsburg empress who came to Innsbruck for the wedding of her son in the eighteenth century. It begins at the Arch of Triumph, which marks her entry into the city, and goes past many impressive buildings to the edge of the "Old Town."

It was on this crescent-shaped plot of ground near the river that the Innsbruck of the Middle Ages stood. It is a network of narrow, winding streets. The walks are covered with arched roofs, or arcades, and the houses have bay windows. Many of the shops can be identified by their beautiful hand-wrought metal signs.

In a little square there stands one of the most beautiful buildings of the later Middle Ages. It is called the "Golden Roof." On the front of the building is a balcony over fifty feet

high, covered by a sharply slanted roof that glows like bright gold in the sun. Three thousand gilded copper tiles cover this roof. The balcony was built about the year 1500 by the Emperor Maximilian, who used it as a "box seat" from which his guests could watch the traveling musicians, jugglers, acrobats, and magicians perform for them in the square below.

THE GOLDEN EAGLE

Nearby stands a hotel called the Golden Eagle. "Sooner or later everybody comes to Tyrol," the Tyrolese say. The history of this hotel shows that they may be right. The hotel is still open for business, and every night its winehouse with the high arched ceiling and jolly accordion players is a scene of merriment. No one knows how old the Golden Eagle is, but it is said that the King of Tunis stopped there in 1548.

Although that seems doubtful, there is evidence that the Emperor Joseph was a guest at the Golden Eagle in 1777 on his return trip to Vienna from Paris, where he had visited his sister, Marie Antoinette. Disguised as a nobleman named Count Falkenstein, he saw the sights of Innsbruck and charmed the townspeople.

Other guests at the Golden Eagle were the poets Johann Wolfgang von Goethe (1786), who loved Tyrol, and Heinrich Heine (1828), who thought the Tyrolese were "idiots." Paganini, the great violinist, cut his initials in the window sill of his room there, proving that geniuses like to be remembered as much as those students who have scratched their names on schoolroom desks.

Andreas Hofer, the hero of the Tyrolean revolt against Napoleon's army, spoke to his troops at the Golden Eagle in 1809. A man who later owned the Golden Eagle made some extra money by selling dozens of pairs of Hofer's "original" boots to easily fooled visitors.

Photographs are often placed on graves in provincial cemeteries.

LOOKING AT INNSBRUCK

Innsbruck's climate is not harsh. Though the Inn Valley nestles among the mountains fifteen hundred feet above sea level, the great North Range that towers six thousand feet above Innsbruck shields it from the strong, cold winds of the north. At the same time, the passes leading up from Italy permit warm southern winds to reach the Inn Valley.

In Innsbruck the mountains seem to change as often as the sea. In the morning they have an incredible freshness, glowing pink under the rising sun. At noon their snowy peaks stand out more clearly than before, and then the mountains darken as day fades. Twilight dyes them a somber blue.

Innsbruck itself is really best at twilight, when you can look out across its rooftops and watch the lights come on in all the old houses. The lights give the buildings a cheerful warmth, and the towers stand out as tall shadowy outlines against the darkening sky. Later at night, the outlines of the mountains are blotted out. Then the lights of the ski lodges near the peaks seem to come from houses suspended in the sky like stars.

MOUNTAIN CLIMBING

The Tyrolese are great walkers, and the mountains around Innsbruck are seen best by going about on foot. A good way to reach the trails is to go by trolley car. From the Maria Theresien-strasse the trolley clatters out of town and, at the edge of the mountains, plunges into the forest. It winds through clumps of evergreen trees, and sometimes the lower branches scrape the top of the car. Perhaps through the window you will see a small deer feeding behind a fallen tree.

When the trolley stops, you will easily find one of the trails to follow; they are clearly marked to direct you safely. The walks lead through rolling meadows and up gentle slopes into forests where the light is always dim. The air is rich with the sharp smells of earth, evergreens, and wild mushrooms. Perhaps the trail will lead you past a breath-taking gorge or to a pretty shrine in honor of the Virgin Mary. Or you may suddenly come upon a small military cemetery where the dead lie under crude crosses, brightened here and there by the photograph of an earnest young soldier, and topped by the heavy helmet he wore when he died.

A group of buildings in the distance is always a welcome sight. It means that there is a village ahead, and there is sure to be a little inn where you can rest for a while and buy a refreshing drink and a slice of apple strudel. If you get tired before a village appears, you will always be able to find one of the little benches set up for weary travelers along the trail. On the back of each bench is a metal plate bearing the name of the person who donated it.

There is one excursion which almost every visitor to Innsbruck takes before he leaves—a trip to the Hafelekar, the crest of the North Range. These mountains tower over Innsbruck like a massive wall. Their peaks are 6,000 feet above Innsbruck, or about 7,500 feet above sea level. A little mountain railway goes part of the way up, and two different aerial cable cars complete the ascent.

From the peak, Innsbruck is only a splotch in the valley below. Planes flying through the valley seem hardly higher than the buildings. But when you turn around and face the other way, the tremendous size of the mountain is overwhelming. The landscape stretching north from the Hafelekar is something like the scene that will lie before the first astronaut who reaches the moon. It is a huge white wasteland. Nothing is in sight except miles and miles of icy peaks, an army of giants thrust up through a sea of glaciers and rock.

Detail from the doors of a hand-painted Tyrolean chest

6

Salzburg

If Tyrol sometimes awes us by its natural grandeur, Salzburg reminds us that man has created beauty too. Though this city grew up in the center of one of Europe's leading salt-mining areas (Salzburg means "Salt City"), its fame is cultural rather than commercial. Its churches, its old buildings, and its mighty fortress are masterpieces of architecture. Even more important, Salzburg is the city of Mozart.

THE ARCHBISHOPS

Salzburg has had an unusual history. Like Vienna, it is located on the site of an ancient Celtic settlement. The Romans occupied the town to mine the salt and gold that were nearby. (A modern Salzburg salt mine is shown here.) Then the barbarians, who had chased out the Romans, were converted to Christianity, and the Catholic Church became the most powerful ruling body in the area. This accounts for the differences between Salzburg and most other European cities. It was ruled not by a noble whose son would inherit the crown, but by an archbishop appointed by the Catholic Church. Because its ruler was appointed, Salzburg escaped many of the battles for power which left other cities in ruins.

The Salzach River runs through the town. On the right bank of the river is a steep hill. At the top of the hill stands

55

an enormous fortress called the Hohensalzburg. When the fortress was built, over nine hundred years ago, it became the residence of the Salzburg archbishops. In the thirteenth century the archbishops were granted the title of prince by the Holy Roman Emperor, giving them great worldly, as well as religious power.

Though the violent wars that swirled through central Europe usually passed Salzburg by, the people of the city were not always happy. There was little religious freedom in Europe, and the "Prince-Archbishops" of Salzburg were especially harsh toward those people who did not worship God as their rulers wished them to. During the fifteenth century the Jews were driven out of the city. In the next century the Protestants who refused to be converted were exiled. Thousands of them fled to Poland and to Protestant countries, and many came to America in 1734, settling near Savannah, Georgia.

The archbishops did a great deal to make the city beautiful, following the baroque style so popular at that time. Baroque architecture is known for a style of building that uses heavy twisted forms and a great deal of ornament. Salzburg Cathedral, which in design is something like St. Peter's Cathedral in Rome, was built in the seventeenth century.

The archbishops were also interested in music. They created an orchestra for the city and encouraged composers to write new music for church festivals and ceremonies. Salzburg soon became a center for splendid music.

MOZART

In the middle of the eighteenth century the leader of the archbishop's orchestra was a man named Leopold Mozart. He and his wife had a daughter named Nannerl, and on January 27, 1756, a son was born—Wolfgang Amadeus Mozart. (Wolfgang is a common name in German-speaking countries, and Amadeus means "Beloved of God.") Little Wolfgang of course

The Hohensalzburg fortress overlooks the Salzach River.

heard music while he was still in his crib, but no one could have imagined what was about to take place in the Mozart home. When he was only three years old, Wolfgang was already trying to play the harpsichord (one of the keyboard instruments widely used before the piano was developed).

Soon afterwards, Leopold Mozart put together a collection of music for his daughter, Nannerl, to play. This collection has been preserved, and on one of the pages still can be read today in Leopold's handwriting: "This minuet was learned by little Wolfgang in his fourth year!"

Having learned to play the harpsichord before he was four, Wolfgang continued to amaze his parents. At five, though he could not yet write his name, he began to compose little tunes, using simple musical symbols to get his ideas down on paper. One day when he was six, he came into a room where his father and a couple of professional musicians were practicing a new piece. Wolfgang picked up the music, which he had never seen before, and played right along with them. All Salzburg soon began to talk about this child prodigy.

In those days, even the best musicians were often poorly rewarded. When Leopold Mozart realized his son's amazing talent, he saw a way to make his family rich. Because Nannerl was only four years older than Wolfgang and also a good musician, he decided to take them on a concert tour together.

Mozart, six years old, after a concert at the Schönbrunn Palace

He called them the "Wonder Children." They went to Vienna, where the children played the harpsichord so well that soon that city was as excited about their skill as Salzburg had been.

Finally, their big moment arrived. They were invited to appear before Emperor Francis I and Empress Maria Theresa. Wolfgang and Nannerl charmed the Habsburg rulers with their marvelous playing and their modest behavior.

Then little Wolfgang amazed them by placing a light cloth over the keyboard and playing a tune although he could not see the keys. (This really was not as hard as it seemed. A good musician does not have to look at the keys to play, just as a good typist can work rapidly while looking down at the material she is copying and not at the typewriter keys.)

The applause in the royal palace was tremendous. Six-year-old Wolfgang was so excited by it all that he climbed up on Maria Theresa's lap and kissed her. The Empress, in turn, was so pleased that she presented Wolfgang with a beautiful suit, complete with a tiny sword, that had been made for a young prince. To Nannerl she gave a white dress, prettily brocaded.

The next year the Mozarts made a "grand tour" of Europe. Wolfgang was seven, Nannerl eleven. Now, they played not only the harpsichord, but also the violin and the organ. In Paris in 1763, they were called to play before King Louis XV at the palace of Versailles. There, dressed in his gorgeous suit with the tiny sword, Wolfgang was so successful that his family was invited to live for a while at the palace.

Moving on to London, the children played for George III, the English king whom the American colonists were soon to fight in the Revolutionary War. Wolfgang, of course, was still a child. Playing the harpsichord before the king one day, he saw a cat come into the room. He stopped playing, jumped up from his stool and ran over to pick up the cat. He petted the purring animal while the royal court burst into laughter.

When he was eight years old, Wolfgang wrote his first symphony. Only a short time before he had been afraid of the loud blaring noise of the horns in the orchestra, but now he was growing up. As he worked on his symphony, he told Nannerl: "Be sure and remind me to give the horns plenty to do."

Later he and his father traveled to Rome, where Wolfgang played before the Pope. The Pope decorated the boy with the Order of the Silver Spur and gave him the title of *Signor Cavaliere*. Wolfgang amused himself writing home to Nannerl and signing the letters with his new title.

These were to be the brightest days of Wolfgang's life, for many misfortunes lay ahead of him. The European tours did not earn as much money as his father had hoped. The nobles applauded and made much of the children, but usually gave them watches and other trinkets instead of money.

When Wolfgang was only fourteen, he was made the director of the archbishop's orchestra at Salzburg. It did not bring him happiness because he felt cramped in the city. Salzburg was too small to give him the opportunity he needed for success, and many of the other musicians were jealous of the boy who had been promoted above them. Wolfgang, a young man now, went on composing music for the church services, but his talent was not appreciated. To make matters worse, there was a new archbishop who did not understand the gifted composer's possibilities and treated him like an ordinary servant. Finally, Wolfgang quarreled with him and left Salzburg to go to Vienna.

Even in Vienna, Wolfgang Mozart's genius was not fully appreciated. Except for the recognition of a few people like Joseph Haydn—another great composer—Mozart was neglected. He was composing some of the most beautiful music ever written—symphonies, comic and serious operas, serenades, and concertos—over six hundred works in all. He was appointed composer for the court of Emperor Joseph II, but he still had to give lessons to earn enough money.

One night, a mysterious stranger knocked on Mozart's door. The man was wrapped in a great gray cloak, and he brought a letter from his master, asking Mozart to compose the music for a Requiem Mass, that is, a mass for the dead. Mozart was very ill and had a strange feeling while writing the piece that it was to be his own Requiem, too.

This proved true, since Mozart never finished the Requiem. For, while he was working on it to earn the money he badly needed, Wolfgang Mozart died on December 5, 1791. He was only thirty-five years old. The day of his burial was cold and rainy. None of his friends thought enough of him to go to the cemetery with his body, and later the gravedigger could not remember where he had dug the grave. Even today, no one knows where Austria's greatest musical genius lies buried.

It was only after his death that the Austrian people began to realize what a wonderful man had lived and died among them. The soul of Mozart seemed to come back to Salzburg and leave its mark on the city. Changes, of course, were taking

Getreidegasse, where Mozart was born, as it looks today

Mozart's Don Giovanni *at the Salzburg Marionette Theater*

place there. The whirlwind created by Napoleon at the beginning of the nineteenth century swept Salzburg out of the archbishops' control and into the hands of Germany. Later it was given to the Habsburgs, along with the beautiful lake country around it which today makes up the province of Salzburg.

THE FESTIVAL

Salzburg is chiefly known as the city of Mozart. Visitors seem to feel the composer's presence there. Music has become a part of the city's atmosphere. Only after World War I, however, was the dream of a festival completely realized. During that terrible war the people of Salzburg had looked forward to a time when the art lovers of the world might "unite in festive delight." The annual Salzburg Festival began in 1920.

Thousands of visitors now pour into the city each summer at festival time. Salzburg has grown to be a city with about

110,000 inhabitants, but it still has its early charm. The tremendous fortress on the hill is still its most prominent building, but the citizens of Salzburg have created a city which keeps visitors' eyes from fastening very long on any one sight. The city's art and architecture are a constant delight. In addition to many paintings and statues in the baroque style, there are others in the later rococo style. The Austrian writer, Count Ferdinand Czernin, has colorfully described this style. "Rococo is just Baroque and a bit of laughter. Fluffy little angels floating about on their own special clouds, Madonnas that might start giggling any moment, statues of hideous gnomes and laughing satyrs standing about the parks. That is Rococo."

People who come to the festival love to wander through this city with its narrow streets, its old inns, and its inviting shops. Each corner seems to present a new adventure. Here the visitor will come upon the house where Mozart was born, in the *Getreidegasse* (Grain Lane). There he will come upon a street with the funny name *Bieryodelgasse* (Beer-Yodel Lane). And again he will find himself standing in front of the *Festspielhaus,* or Festival Playhouse, which was once a stable for the archbishops' horses and is now the scene of many of the festival events.

What happens at the festival? Of course, there are concerts, operas, and plays. One of the most colorful of the plays is *Everyman,* which is presented each year in the square in front of the cathedral. The spectators are thrilled by the many strange effects during the play, such as ghostly voices coming from the white marble façade (front) of the cathedral, and even from as far away as the huge fortress on the hill. And of course there is the wonderful music of Mozart. Though he was often unhappy in this city, it would please him to know that his music not only lives on there but in a very real sense makes Salzburg one of the living centers of world culture. It is truly Mozart's spirit which lies behind the festival.

Two views of Vorarlberg mountains: above, a backdrop for a peaceful farming village; below, a setting for "the white art"

7

Six Provinces

Austria, as we have said, is made up of nine *laender*, or provinces, in the same way that the United States is made up of fifty states. The nine Austrian provinces are Vienna, Tyrol, Salzburg, Vorarlberg, Carinthia, Styria, Upper Austria, Lower Austria, and Burgenland.

We have already looked at Vienna, Tyrol, and Salzburg. However, to discuss those three areas and neglect the rest would be as unfair as if a foreigner came to America and tried to describe it by writing only about New York, Texas, and Washington, D.C. Such a book would give a very incomplete idea of the United States. Thus we must look at the other provinces, too, to get a true picture of Austria.

VORARLBERG, THE RHINE PROVINCE

Like Austria itself, the province of Vorarlberg is a land of mountains and rivers. Lying between Switzerland and Tyrol, it is Austria's gateway to the west. Its river is the Rhine, not the Danube. The Rhine rises in Switzerland, flows north along the western side of Vorarlberg and enters Lake Constance near the northwest corner of the province.

Lake Constance (*Bodensee* in German) belongs to three countries. Its waters lap the shores of Austria, Switzerland, and

West Germany, and it is one of the most beautiful lakes in Europe. Bregenz, the capital of the province of Vorarlberg, lies on the lake's eastern rim, with the peaks of the Swiss and Vorarlberg Alps in the distance. At the yearly festival which is held in Bregenz, thousands of people watch the "Play on the Lake," a performance on a huge stage that floats on the quiet waters of Lake Constance.

Another of Vorarlberg's towns is Bludenz, which lies on the Ill River. During the Middle Ages a duke called "Frederick of the Empty Pockets" lived here. His emblem was the unicorn, an imaginary white, horselike animal which had a single long horn growing out of its forehead. The unicorn is now the town emblem. The duke quarreled with both the Pope and the emperor, and for a time he was in a lot of trouble, as his nickname tells you. Fortunately for him, the people of Bludenz supported him, and at last he regained the land and the wealth which were rightfully his. His son, in fact, came to be called the "Prince of Many Coins." Today Bludenz is a pretty town with a church and a castle. Its narrow streets seem hardly to have changed since the Middle Ages.

Many of the people of the province make fine cloth and lace by hand. In its quiet villages they wear the colorful costumes that have been traditional there for hundreds of years. There is, for instance, the *schapel*. This is a large, ornate headdress made of gold and silver wire and covered with bits of colored glass, pearls, and colorful embroidery. Each headdress has been handed down from mother to daughter, and is worn by a village girl on holidays. There is a different model *schapel* in each valley.

The mountains are everywhere in Vorarlberg. The people of this province love them, but they are afraid of them too. Little villages that lie at the bottoms of steep slopes are in great danger when there has been a heavy fall of snow, for the slightest commotion can bring an avalanche down on top of them.

An avalanche builds up such terrific force that it compresses and pushes the air ahead of it, so that the air can splinter trees and houses a hundred feet in front of the avalanche itself. After it has passed, a vacuum is created because there is no air, and then people who have escaped the avalanche may be sucked out of their homes by the vacuum.

But the mountains help man too. They rise to great heights in Vorarlberg, especially in the south where the peaks are over ten thousand feet high. Here great hydroelectric dams have been built to harness the power of the mountain streams. The dams provide electricity (which the people call "white coal") for homes and factories.

And of course, the mountains of Vorarlberg provide vast areas for "the white art," which is what the people call skiing. Like Tyrol, Vorarlberg has become a playland for the enthusiastic skiers of Europe. So tiny that it is known in Austria as the "Little Province," Vorarlberg has more tourist attractions than places many times its size.

CARINTHIA, THE SOUTHERN PROVINCE

Carinthia is Austria's southern province. On the south it is bordered by Italy and Yugoslavia. It lies on the age-old route between Vienna and Venice, Italy.

In Carinthia are the sunlight and warmth which attract people from the cloudy, chilly north. Carinthia is a land of two hundred lakes, and in their clear, warm waters the Austrian people forget for a time about skiing and ice skating to enjoy swimming and boating. Lake Wörther is the most fashionable of Carinthia's lakes. On its shores are tennis courts, golf courses, and charming towns where flower carnivals add to the gaiety.

More secluded is Lake Millstatt, which lies in the bed of an Ice-Age glacier. Overlooking the lake is a Benedictine monastery, whose church was built in the eleventh century.

Sticks and rocks keep these roofs from blowing away in the strong Alpine winds. The mountain in the distance is the Grossglockner.

Nearby is a lime tree which is over one thousand years old. Like so much of Austria, Carinthia has been cultivated by man for thousands of years.

The province is encircled by mountains. On them grow thick forests of birch and pine trees, which are cut for lumber. Lumbering, with iron mining, has long been one of Carinthia's principal industries. In the mountains in the northwest corner of the province, a breath-taking road skirts the Grossglockner, a 12,454-foot peak which is Austria's highest.

Carinthia's capital is Klagenfurt, a prosperous market and resort town on the Glan River near Lake Wörther. On market days the farmers bring in their produce from the countryside, and the sunny outdoor market is filled with ripe fruits and vegetables. Near the fountains in the town square stands an impressive stone statue of a winged dragon—Klagenfurt's official emblem.

There are many other sights to see among the city's fine old churches, museums, and official buildings. But if the sun is warm, and the tour around Klagenfurt begins to tire you, the beach is never very far away. A swim in Lake Wörther is a favorite Carinthian remedy for too much sight-seeing!

STYRIA, THE GREEN PROVINCE

Styria, called the "Green Province" because of its lovely meadows and forests, is probably less visited by foreigners than any other section of Austria. It is remarkable that this is so. Perhaps it is because Styria lies in the southeast corner of Austria, far from the path of most of the tourists, who hurry about between the big capital cities of western and central Europe.

The Erzberg (Ore Mountain) is one of Styria's marvels. Rising 2,500 feet in the air, it is almost a solid mass of iron ore, and has been mined since before the time of the Romans. The mountain's rust-colored sides have been carved into thirty great shelves, each of them 70 feet high and 2,100 feet long. On these shelves the miners, assisted now by modern cranes and machines, still gather the ore in much the same way their ancestors did. Even at the present rapid rate of mining, there is enough ore left in the mountain to last for another hundred years.

Graz, the capital of Styria province, has a population of about 240,000, which makes it the second largest city in Austria. (Vienna, of course, is the biggest.) This busy city still holds much of its old charm. The bell in the huge clock tower has been tolling to announce danger or festivals to the people of Graz since 1587. In Graz, you can see men wearing the gray suits with green lapels and broad green trouser stripes which have become a sort of national costume all over Austria.

Styria has many lovely small towns, too. One of the most famous is Mariazell, where pilgrims flock to pray to the Virgin Mary. According to an old legend, the town was founded by a monk who had lost his way in the vast mountainous area of the Hochschwab. He had given up hope of ever finding his way to safety. Then he remembered a picture of the Mother of Christ which he had been carrying. He took it out, and prayed to her for help. Suddenly, a path opened in the rocks ahead of him. Arriving safely at the bottom of the mountain, he built a monk's shelter for himself so that he could stay there to honor Mary. It is said that this shelter, or cell, has grown into the town of Mariazell, which means "Mary's Cell."

Years of surface mining have carved terraces on the Erzberg slopes.

The Lady Altar in the church at Mariazell

In southern Styria there are many vineyards on the hillsides. There, as the grapes ripen in the warm sun, flocks of birds, such as starlings and thrushes, come to eat them. To protect their grapes the people place wooden rattles among the vines. When a gust of wind comes along, all the rattles begin to make a clatter at once, and the birds rise up and fly away. But they are not fooled for long, and they soon settle down again on the heavily laden vines. All through the summer afternoons the silence is broken now and again by the sound of hundreds of rattles, tapping out their warning in vain, for all around the birds continue to feast on their share of the sweet Styrian grapes.

A religious procession on Lake Hallstatt

UPPER AUSTRIA,
THE PLAYGROUND PROVINCE

The province of Upper Austria is another of Europe's most attractive summer playgrounds. The Salzkammergut region is a wonderland of mountains, lakes, and villages. The lakes are especially popular, and almost all of them have histories that go back a long, long time.

There is the Mondsee (Moon Lake), where delicate water lilies float on its quiet blue surface. Traces of ancient houses, called pile-dwellings, have been found there. These houses were built on stilts along the shores of the lake over 2,500 years before Christ. Rising straight up from the lake itself is a tremendous mass of rock, which is called the "Dragon's Wall."

An old legend tells us how, in the eighth century, the lake got its name. One night, a duke named Odilo went hunting in the hills behind the Dragon's Wall. The moon had been covered by clouds, and the duke was lost in the darkness. He began to feel his way along a rocky path. Just as he was about to step over the edge of the cliff and plunge to his death, the moon suddenly burst through the clouds. Then he saw, glistening in the moonlight far below him, the rippled surface of the lake. He named the waters Moon Lake.

There were ancient settlements around Lake Hallstatt, too. The banks of this lake drop sharply to great depths, so there were no pile-dwellings here. But many valuable relics have been found in the graves of prehistoric men who made their homes nearby. The town of Hallstatt, on the shore of the lake, is the oldest community in Austria. Salt deposits nearby have been worked for at least 4,500 years. At one time the people of Hallstatt earned their living by trading salt to the Romans for products made elsewhere in the empire. Today colorful religious processions take place in boats on the lake because there is not enough land to hold parades between the lake and the mountains.

Linz, one of Austria's most productive industrial cities

The Kremsmunster Monastery, one of Europe's most famous, is in Upper Austria. It was originally built in the year 777, by Duke Tassilo. It is said that on this spot Tassilo's son, while out hunting, had been gored to death by a wild boar, and the monastery was built in the boy's memory. Repaired many times since, it has never lost its beauty. There you can see its famous fish tank, which is surrounded by a covered arcade and so designed that the reflection of the sky makes marvelous patterns in the water. The monastery also has an eight-story observatory from which the stars can be watched by astronomers. There are also old paintings of the Holy Roman Emperors and a library with over ninety thousand valuable books.

But Upper Austria is more than a tourist's paradise. Its cities are among the most productive in the country. Linz, its provincial capital, has a population of 197,000. It is a busy port on the Danube River. Steyr is a world-famous manufacturing center which turns out bicycles, automobiles, farm machinery, and other iron and steel products.

LOWER AUSTRIA, THE RICH PROVINCE

Lower Austria (Nieder-Österreich) surrounds the city of Vienna, which is a province in itself. Vienna, then, serves as the national capital of Austria, the provincial capital of Vienna, and the provincial capital of Lower Austria. When you leave the city of Vienna in any direction, you enter Lower Austria, and for most of the Viennese it is a favorite year-round playground.

Lower Austria is the country's largest and most productive province. Everywhere you look you will see things growing. The fields are thickly covered with corn and wheat; most of the country's grain comes from here. Its vineyards produce the grapes from which many fine wines are made. In its orchards grow all sorts of fruits and nuts, among them peaches, apricots, cherries, and chestnuts.

In the Marchfeld plains east of Vienna are miles and miles of oil derricks. This is one of Europe's richest oil fields. From these oil wells Austria takes all the petroleum it needs and has enough left over to export at a profit. It is the only European country outside the Iron Curtain that is able to do this.

One of the favorite vacation regions of Lower Austria is the beautiful Wachau Valley. The Danube River flows through this valley, and here are found story-book villages and world-famous buildings. Along this stretch of the Danube stood Duernstein Castle, where King Richard the Lionhearted of England was held prisoner. The castle was destroyed by Swedish soldiers during the Thirty Years' War in the seventeenth century, but its ruins can still be seen towering above the little town of Duernstein.

Another splendid building along the Danube is the Melk Monastery. It was on this site that the Babenberg family, which

Oil derricks on the Marchfeld Plain

ruled Austria before the Habsburgs, built their castle around
the year 1000. When the Babenbergs moved eastward toward
Vienna, they turned the castle over to the Benedictine monks
to use as a monastery. It was rebuilt in the baroque style during
the eighteenth century. The beautiful Melk Monastery is one
of the reasons why the Viennese think that their Lower Austria
is a very special place.

Grape pickers in Lower Austria strap on these wooden baskets.

BURGENLAND, THE EASTERN PROVINCE

Within the provincial borders of Burgenland lies one of the most remarkable lakes in the world. Here, on the far eastern border of Austria where the Alps begin to level out into the plains of eastern Europe, Neusiedler Lake continues to amaze both tourists and scientists. The lake is twenty miles long and five miles wide, but nowhere is the water in it more than five feet deep!

For the most part, Neusiedler Lake reaches a depth of only three feet. Anyone can easily wade all the way across it. It is, nevertheless, a favorite lake for vacationists. Flat-bottomed boats are specially built to glide along its surface. In a thick band of reeds around the lake nests the greatest variety of water birds in Europe—herons, ducks, and other birds with strange names like the bustard and the bearded titmouse.

Nobody knows where the water of the lake comes from. Only one stream flows into it, and that stream does not carry enough water to supply so large a lake. About once every seventy years, Neusiedler Lake simply dries up, and its water completely disappears. Not a trace of it remains, except for a muddy hole in the ground! Fortunately, it always fills up again, just as mysteriously.

Burgenland was a part of the old Habsburg empire, and most of its people were German-speaking, but it always lay within the kingdom of Hungary. After World War I, however, it joined the new Austrian Republic. Its provincial capital, Eisenstadt, was for a long time the home of the great composer, Joseph Haydn. He is buried in the church there.

But perhaps the town that will interest you most is Rust, near Neusiedler Lake. There, on rooftops all over town, you will see the huge, round nests of the white stork. The stork is Europe's favorite bird and, judging from the number of them in Rust, this must be the stork's favorite town!

Vikar Josef Mohr schuf hier den Text des Liedes.

Stille Nacht / Heilige Nacht

Oberndorf

Hier stand die alte Pfarrkirche / in welcher das Lied 1818 das erstemal zur Christmette gesungen wurde.

Stifter: Ostmärkischer Sängerbund Wien 1933

Josef Mohr

geb. den 11. Dez. 1792 zu Salzburg / von 1817 bis 1819 Hilfspriester in Oberndorf / starb den 5. Dez. 1848 als Pfarr-Vikar in Wagrain.

8

Land of Music

In 1787, three wonderful composers were living in Vienna. They knew one another and admired one another's music. The young Beethoven had come there to ask Mozart to be his teacher, but Beethoven soon had to go home to Germany because of his mother's illness. When he returned to Vienna five years later, Mozart was dead, and Beethoven went to Haydn for guidance. A man who loved music once wrote: "Beethoven received Mozart's spirit from Haydn's hands."

It is not surprising that this took place in Vienna. For hundreds of years the most famous musicians in the world have gone there to work. No other city has played so important a part in the development of music.

This joy in music and the ability to create it have always been a part of the Austrian people. Austria, in fact, has been called the "Land of Music." Even today people in lonely Alpine villages take pleasure in playing the old songs, and sometimes they make up new words and music as they go along. They play the violin, the flute, and the zither. Even the old instruments are still played, such as the *Hoelzernes Glachter,* which means "laughter of the wood" and is similar to a xylophone.

A stained-glass window commemorates Father Mohr.

Music is not a dull pastime to the Austrians. It makes them gay, and this gaiety appears in places where the rest of the world is usually very solemn. Listen to this Tyrolean carol, written to be sung to the Christ Child at Christmastime:

> So came we running to the crib,
>   I and also you,
> A beeline into Bethlehem,
>   Hopsa, trala loo:
> "O, baby dear, take anything
>   Of all the little gifts we bring:
> Have apples or have butter,
>   Maybe pears or yellow cheese;
> Or would you rather have some nuts,
>   Or plums, or what you please.
> Alleluja, alleluja;
>   Alle—, alle—, alleluja."

We can trace the Austrian love for music back to the twelfth century, when a visitor said of the country: "Here the poor and rich dance and fiddle." The church has always encouraged music. The emperors, too, encouraged music by organizing the Vienna Choir Boys to sing at religious ceremonies, and by bringing Europe's finest composers and musicians to their palaces. By the eighteenth century, a person could hear the best music in the world by going to Vienna.

JOSEPH HAYDN, THE BELOVED MUSICIAN

Not every musician had to go there from some distant land. Joseph Haydn was born nearby in the Vienna Woods on March 31, 1732. As a small boy he was brought to Vienna to sing in a church choir. When his voice changed, the choirmaster turned him out into the street. Young Haydn was forced to spend a cold night outdoors before strangers took him in and gave him food and shelter.

Soon people began to hear about this young man who could compose such beautiful tunes. A prince named Esterhazy asked Haydn to come to his castle in Burgenland (then in Hungary) to be his court composer. Haydn accepted.

Esterhazy's castle was at Eisenstadt, near Neusiedler Lake. Haydn was happy there. He lived a quiet life, writing music and learning more about his art. As his chamber music and symphonies were performed over the years, he came to be recognized as one of the greatest composers of his time.

He is said to have been the best-loved composer in the history of music. Born of a peasant family, Haydn used the folk tunes of central Europe in his own compositions, decorating them and putting new life into them so that they were fresh and strong in his long symphonies. But even when world-wide fame came to him he remained a modest man.

Few older people have the ability to learn from the young. Haydn was twenty-four years older than Mozart. As a boy, Mozart had heard Haydn's music, loved it, and learned from it. Later, in Vienna, Haydn listened to Mozart's music and realized that he could learn much from the young man. He was one of the few musicians of his time who was not jealous of Mozart.

When Haydn received an offer from the city of Prague to write a symphony for a special ceremony, he replied that this honor should go to Mozart. "It would hardly be possible for anyone to stand beside the great Mozart," he wrote.

Haydn, known as the father of the symphony, composed one hundred and four of them. Many of them have nicknames: the *Toy Symphony*, the *Surprise Symphony*, and the *Clock Symphony*. Yet, when Mozart died, it was Haydn who said of him: "He was a truly great musician. Friends often flatter me that I have some genius, but Mozart stood far above me."

It isn't often that a famous man speaks of his rivals with so much sincerity and generosity. No wonder then, that when he died in 1809, all Austria mourned him. Yet some of his admirers did a queer thing after he had been buried at Eisenstadt. They removed the old man's head from his casket. It was not until 1954, 150 years after his death, that the matter was set right. A strange funeral procession moved slowly into Burgenland from Vienna, carrying Haydn's skull, which was then buried with his body again in the old church at Eisenstadt. Today, his music is still widely played, and is loved by people of all ages.

BEETHOVEN

Now both Mozart and Haydn were dead, but Vienna still claimed the man whom some believe to be the greatest composer of them all. Though his first trip to Vienna had been brief, Ludwig van Beethoven was determined to go back there. Leaving Germany again in 1792, he studied for a time under Haydn in Vienna. Beethoven was a fun-loving man at heart, and he liked people and parties. The Viennese, who had treated Mozart badly, made up for it in their treatment of Beethoven. They knew he was a wonderful musician.

A great deal of sadness came into Beethoven's life for, while still a young man, he began to lose his hearing. He grew self-

Beethoven's home in Vienna

conscious about it, because he could no longer take part in the conversations that he loved. Soon he was completely deaf. He no longer went to visit people, and he was forced to give up his career as a concert pianist. He became a solitary, lonely person. But by now he was already a master of musical form.

"What humiliation," he wrote, "when someone is standing near me and he hears a far-off flute and I cannot hear it; or when he hears a shepherd singing and I can hear nothing. Such things carried me close to despair."

Now, only his work brought him relief from unhappiness. As he sank deeper into his deafness and his solitude, he began to speak to the world through his beautiful compositions. When we hear this music we find it almost impossible to believe that it was written by a deaf man.

Beethoven loved Vienna and the countryside around it. He stayed on in the city in 1809, when it was attacked by Napoleon's army. When the barrage was at its heaviest, Beethoven took shelter in the cellar of his brother's home.

Worn out by illness, Beethoven died in 1827. His *Eroica Symphony, Fifth Symphony, Choral Symphony, Moonlight Sonata,* and his last quartets are among the greatest works ever composed. During a life of suffering he wrote music that has helped people all over the world to endure their sufferings.

SCHUBERT AND STRAUSS

Vienna continued to be the music capital of the world. Franz Schubert followed in Beethoven's footsteps. Although he lived to be only thirty-two, he wrote nine symphonies, much chamber music, and six hundred beautiful songs. His last symphony, which was never finished, was not discovered until fifty years after his death. It is famous now as the *Unfinished Symphony.* Schubert was a great admirer of Beethoven and, though he had met him only briefly, he asked to be buried as close as possible to the great master's grave.

Lighter music, too, found its home in Vienna. Johann Strauss, who was the son of a famous Viennese musician, became even more successful than his father. His waltzes and operettas are still popular all over the world. The "Waltz King," as he was called, wrote the "Emperor Waltz," "The Blue Danube," and "Tales from the Vienna Woods."

In 1876, Strauss was invited to the United States to take part in the celebration which marked the one hundredth anniversary of the Declaration of Independence. At Boston he conducted a huge orchestra and chorus, numbering several thousand people.

"It was very difficult," he said afterwards. "Since we all started playing and singing together, I tried to get everybody to *finish* together too."

FATHER MOHR'S "SILENT NIGHT"

Probably no piece of Austrian music is so well-known as the Christmas carol, "Silent Night." It was composed in the little village of Oberndorf, near Salzburg, in 1818. At Christmastime that year the people of Oberndorf were saddened to learn that their church organ had broken down. They were afraid that there would be no music in the church on Christmas Eve. Then the parish priest, Father Joseph Mohr, decided that he must try to do something to make up for the organ's loss.

Earlier, on December 24, he had visited a woman whose child was ill. Father Mohr kept in his mind the vivid picture of the mother and her child and wrote out the words for a Christmas song. Then he took the song to a musician named Franz Gruber, who added music. At Mass on Christmas Eve the people of Oberndorf heard the new song performed by the choir to the accompaniment of a guitar.

For some years the song lay hidden with other music in the old church. It was found one day by someone who liked it and took it to the Rainers, a family of Tyrolean singers. In 1839, the Rainers made a tour of America and the song, which was a part of their performance, delighted those who heard it. Translated into English, it was called "Silent Night"—today one of the best-known of all Christmas carols.

A LIVING TRADITION

The musical tradition has stayed alive in Austria down to our own times. Its roots are just where they began—in religion and in the countryside. Even yodeling, which probably developed from the cattle calls used by cowherds in the mountains, has many uses. Yodeling usually sounds comic to Americans, but it can be very tender, and sometimes the country people use it as a background for Christmas carols.

Vienna has two opera houses where performances can be heard every night for ten months of the year. You can go to the opera for as little as thirty cents. Vienna has a world-famous philharmonic orchestra and an excellent symphony orchestra. Each provincial capital and many of the smaller towns and cities in Austria have fine orchestras of their own.

LEFT: *Costumed villagers dance the Bandl Tanz in Mariazell*
RIGHT: *Herbert von Karajan and the Vienna Philharmonic*

9

Religion and the Arts

Life, for the Austrians, is a many-sided experience. Because they are a religious people, they bring their religion into most of the activities of everyday living. You can see examples of this not just in the churches, but everywhere in the cities and villages and countryside. Religion contributes to the outer, as well as to the inner, richness of Austrian life.

INFLUENCE OF THE ROMAN CATHOLIC RELIGION

About nine out of every ten Austrians are Roman Catholics; most of the rest are Lutherans. Signs and symbols, then, of the Catholic Church are seen all over the country. Huge cathedrals are commonly the most prominent landmarks in the cities. The needle- or onion-shaped spire of the parish church is always the first sign you see on approaching a village, just as at sea a mast sticking up over the horizon is the first sign of a ship that is coming into view.

Homes and buildings are decorated with crucifixes and holy pictures. Along the broad highways or the narrowest mountain paths are pretty little statues or small shrines like the one shown on the opposite page, dedicated to Jesus, Mary, or to some favorite saint of the region. The gaiety with which the Austrians approach certain holy days sometimes leads strangers to believe that they do not take their religion seriously. On the contrary, most of them do take it very seriously. This is why they have such a good time celebrating the principal feast days of their church.

The Austrians love music and processions, and the many holy days of the year provide them with good excuses for plenty of both. As the New Year is rung in (New Year's Day is also a Catholic holy day), small brass bands often play in church towers in villages throughout the Alps. On January 6— the Feast of the Epiphany—the children celebrate the revelation of Christ to the Magi, or Three Wise Men. The children go from house to house, dressed as Magi, carrying a pole with the star of Bethlehem pinned to its top.

Lent is a season of fasting for the Austrians, as it is for Catholics throughout the world. At one time the Church forbade the eating of many more foods during Lent than it does now, and the people had to look around for tidbits that satisfied their hunger without breaking any of the Church's rules. A favorite snack was the pretzel. Its very form was intended to remind the people of their religion, for it was made in the image of two arms crossed in devotion. The pretzel is still made in that shape today.

Eggs, a popular Austrian dish, were forbidden during Lent. The eggs accumulated during this time, for hens do not follow Church rules. On Easter morning, when Lent ended, the people painted eggs with bright colors and gave them to their children, relatives, and friends. They made a welcome gift, for none had been eaten since the beginning of Lent, six weeks before. Now, at Eastertime, you can see baskets of gaily colored eggs standing on tables in village restaurants. Some of them are quite fancy. They are colored and then wrapped in ferns. When they are boiled, delicate, lacy patterns form on their shells.

Austrian children in costume for the Feast of Epiphany

Easter is a time of processions. In many Austrian towns the people decorate their horses with flowers and gay ribbons, and ride them out into the fields. When this custom began, it was purely a religious ceremony to make the fields more fruitful during the coming year. Later the people continued the ride as a pleasant celebration of the holy day, and it became what we now call the "Easter Parade."

Many of these customs began in pagan times and were kept and changed a little by the people when they became Christians. Other pagan customs have not been changed at all. In the spring, for instance, the peasants in some places parade out into the fields, beating the earth with long crackling whips, ringing cowbells, pounding drums, and blowing trumpets to frighten winter away. The peasants themselves wear horrible masks, both to "frighten" winter and to keep winter from recognizing them and getting his revenge later on. Today, some of these celebrations have become popular tourist attractions.

The most colorful time of the year in Austria is when Christmas is coming. Then there are all sorts of religious festivities. One of them is St. Barbara's Day, December 4, when many girls break off the branch of a cherry tree and take it inside, where they keep it in water. If the branch bursts into bloom exactly on Christmas Eve, it is a sign that the girl will find a good husband during the coming year. If it blooms at some other time, it still makes a colorful Christmas decoration!

December 6 is St. Nicholas' Day in Austria. St. Nicholas was a famous bishop of the Middle Ages. He became the patron saint of children and is the original of the American Santa Claus. The Austrians have a ceremony in which the children of the town are brought before two men—one of them is "St. Nicholas" and the other an impish man named Krampus. There is a great deal of fun as Krampus tries to hit the children with his rod and St. Nicholas drives him away. Then the children all promise to be good until Christmas.

It is the Christ Child, not Santa Claus, who gives the children their presents on Christmas Eve. The presents are left under the Christmas tree, which is a small pine or fir, usually lighted by candles rather than by electric bulbs. In German, the Christ Child is *Christkindel*. When Austrian and German immigrants first came to America they spoke of a *Christkindel* at Christmastime. The word was twisted a bit by the English-speaking people to "Kriss Kringle," which is sometimes used as another name for the American Santa Claus.

Christmas is very gay in Austria. There are processions and caroling ("Silent Night," of course, is the favorite carol) and lots of visiting with friends and relatives. Everybody eats a big dinner, and there are all kinds of cakes and cookies. Everybody goes to church, for the Austrians know that Christmas, first of all, is a religious holiday.

POETRY AND ARCHITECTURE

Many Americans speak of the arts as being important, although they turn to them only when they have nothing else to do. However, if you have any doubts about how much the arts mean to the Austrians, you must remember the actions

Priests carry willow branches to St. Stephen's on Palm Sunday.

of the Viennese after World War II. Though their city was in ruins and they did not have enough to eat, the Viennese spent their last coins to buy tickets for their favorite plays, symphonies, and operas. Art is a part of the Austrian way of life.

Since music is so deeply woven into the lives of the people, is it not surprising to discover that Austria's most famous poet is still thought of mainly as a "singer of songs." He was Walther von der Vogelweide, and he was born in Tyrol about 1170.

Sir Walther was a poor knight who truly had to sing for his supper. Traveling with bands of clowns, jugglers, and magicians, he visited the castles of the Austrian nobles and made up songs which he sang to them in exchange for his meals and a bed. Often he was too poor to buy the necessities of life. A letter that has come down to us tells about a bishop who gave Sir Walther some money in 1203 "to buy himself a fur coat against the winter cold."

He wrote some of the most beautiful love poems of all time. One of them, "Under the Lindens," is still popular in German-speaking countries. It is a simple poem about a girl who meets her favorite boy under a linden tree, and it ends:

> Not a soul could see save I and he,
> And a certain small brown bird:
> Tandaradei,
> Trust him not to breathe a word.

Like most great poets, he was ahead of his time in his beliefs. All around him people were killing other people because they worshiped God in a different way. But Sir Walther wrote:

> Christians, Jews and heathens, serve they all,
> And God has all creation in his care.

After he had wandered the country for twenty-five years, the emperor rewarded him for his beautiful poems and songs by giving him a small estate. Sir Walther settled down there and prepared for death. His will was simple: "To the envious I leave my bad luck; to the liars my sorrow; to false lovers my follies; to the ladies my heart's pain."

Today, in a little park beside the river at Innsbruck, is a statue of Walther von der Vogelweide. He was Austria's greatest poet.

Austria has continued to produce fine poets and writers all the way down to our own time. During the nineteenth century, Franz Grillparzer wrote poems and plays that thrilled his countrymen. In this century, Franz Werfel wrote some excellent books, including *Song of Bernadette*.

Beautiful buildings have long been a part of Austria's scene. The early palaces were built by the emperors, the nobles, and the bishops. Later on the people in the Austrian cities and villages also donated money to erect impressive buildings and other works of art, such as fountains, statues, and arches.

One of the most famous works in Vienna is the Donner Fountain. It was designed by Raphael Donner over two hundred years ago and paid for by Viennese businessmen. Raphael Donner, a poor boy, entered a monastery. There he sang in the choir and secretly collected the wax which had dripped from the chapel candles. Late at night when the others were asleep, the boy molded the wax into lovely little statues. He grew up to become one of Austria's finest sculptors.

Johann Wolfgang von Goethe, the great German poet who is so popular in Austria, once wrote: "The final effect of true art is the feeling of charm." For a thousand years Austrian artists—poets, composers, painters, architects, and sculptors—have been able to charm their appreciative countrymen and, indeed, art lovers throughout the world.

10

Gifts of the Land

"It is only when we are aware of the earth, and of the earth as poetry, that we truly live." These words were written by the American naturalist, Henry Beston, but they could just as easily have been written by an Austrian. The Austrian does not see his beautiful country simply as a series of "views" that will look impressive on picture post cards. He is aware of the endless strength of the earth, and from it he takes new strength for himself.

AUSTRIA'S BIRDS

Birds, to the Austrians, are essential creatures of the earth's poetry. There are no more graceful birds in flight than the swallows, and they may be seen in many parts of Austria. They are sometimes called "Mary's Birds," after the Virgin Mary. It is popularly believed that they arrive in Austria from the south on March 25, the holy day of the Feast of the Annunciation, and leave again at the end of summer on the

Storks, symbols of good luck, are encouraged to nest on rooftops.

Feast of Mary's Birthday, which is September 8. There is a little Austrian song that goes like this:

> It's Blessed Virgin's Birthday,
> The swallows do depart;
> Far to the South they fly away,
> And sadness fills my heart.
> But after snow and ice and rain
> They will in March return again.

A few years ago, a terrible cold wave hit Austria before these little birds had started to leave for the south. Thousands of them were frozen to death, and others, unable to find food, lay helpless on the ground. The Austrian people went out into the cold with baskets on their arms and picked up the swallows. Over ninety thousand birds were saved. The people took them into their homes and barns, fed them, and kept them warm. Later the birds were put in crates and sent by air transport over the Alps to Italy. There they were turned loose again and allowed to continue their migration to the south.

Another favorite bird in Austria is the stork, a large white bird with some black on its tail feathers, a long red bill, a long curved neck, and very long legs. It is over three feet tall. Because storks are said to bring good luck, people encourage them to make nests. The sight of storks nesting on buildings in the Burgenland town of Rust is one that is never forgotten.

Storks like to build their nests in high places, and you can usually find a nest in the clock tower of a church. People sometimes place wagon wheels on their roofs to provide solid foundations on which the storks can build. The nests, which measure as much as six feet across, are made of sticks and twigs, and are lined with straw, leaves, grass, and even paper. There the storks lay their eggs and bring up their families. In the fall they fly to Africa, but they usually return to the same town in the spring.

The bicycle race around Austria is an annual event.

MOUNTAIN SPORTS

One of the happiest sights in Austria is that of a group of
ruddy-faced youngsters, knapsacks on their backs and heavy
boots on their feet, tramping along a mountain trail, laughing
and singing their lively songs. Climbing the peaks, hiking
through the mountains, swimming in the lakes, skating on the
frozen ponds, and fishing in the swift-running streams, Austrians
of all ages enjoy their land. Few people in the world get as
much fun out of their country's natural wonders as do the
Austrians.

Skiing, which is usually thought of first when Austrian sports
are mentioned, became popular there only in this century. The
ski is really a Scandinavian invention. Sixty years ago, wealthy
Swedes and Norwegians would go to the Austrian Alps to test
their skill on the steep hills.

An Austrian boy named Hannes Schneider, who lived in the village of St. Anton am Arlberg, was fascinated by this sport. He made a pair of skis for for himself out of the runners from an old sleigh. A wealthy German, seeing how skillful the boy had become, gave him a real pair of skis. In 1907, Hannes was hired by a St. Anton hotel owner to teach skiing to the hotel's guests. It was then that he began to develop the new methods of skiing which have made the sport so popular everywhere in the world. Hannes Schneider is considered the father of Austrian skiing.

Since that time Austria has produced an astonishing number of famous skiers. Toni Sailer (pronounced ZYLER) was a handsome boy who came from Kitzbühel. Even before the Olympics, he was known for his skiing, and people called him the "Blitz from Kitz." In 1956 the Russians made a great effort to win the Olympic Games. None of them, however, gave as magnificent a performance as did Sailer. This graceful athlete, then twenty

A large crowd has turned out for this sleigh race at Schladming.

years old, performed so naturally that one would have thought he had been born on a pair of skis. "He is gentle with snow," one expert said of Toni, describing his effortless style. When the Olympics began (they were held at Cortina in Italy that year), Toni easily took command of the ski events by winning the Giant Slalom and then the Special Slalom.

The Downhill Race was much tougher. Treacherous ice and fierce winds knocked twenty-five of the seventy-five competitors out of the race. But Toni Sailer remained on his feet and finished well ahead of everybody else. He had won the Gold Medal in all three of the major events. Later, this handsome boy became an Austrian movie star, but he will always be remembered first in his country as one of the greatest of all Olympic athletes.

FOOD AND DRINK

Austria, like France, is noted for its good food. It is one of the few countries in which you do not have to go to an expensive restaurant to get an excellent meal. Austria's more expensive restaurants, in fact, are likely to be only copies of French ones. But in the cheaper places, you will find the same kind of healthful, tasty food that is served in an Austrian's home.

Though Austria does not have large areas of farmland, it is able to produce much of its own food and drink. Austrian wines, which are made from grapes grown in the eastern and southern parts of the country, are among the best in Europe. And the milk from her well-fed cows is as rich as any you will ever taste.

Coffee is one of the few popular products that Austria has to import. This drink is very much a part of the people's way of life. Franz Schubert, the composer, used to grind his own coffee; he claimed that many of his most beautiful melodies came to him as he listened to the sound of the grinding, and so he jokingly called his coffee grinder the "House of the Holy Spirit."

Austria, of course, has no ocean coast line, and so she has to import sea food. Still, many of her fresh-water fish are good eating, too. Trout are plentiful in the Alpine streams and rivers; pike and carp also come from Austrian waters.

Some favorite Austrian dishes are popular in the United States, too. You have probably heard of *Wiener schnitzel,* which the Austrians think of in the same way that Americans think of beefsteak. *Wiener schnitzel* is a thin lean piece of veal, dipped in egg and bread crumbs and fried to a deep golden brown. It is served with a slice of lemon. The Austrians say that the *Wiener schnitzel* should cover your plate, and that you should be able to slip a knife between the golden-brown coating and the meat itself.

A favorite dish in the Alpine areas is *Tiroler groestl.* This is something like hash, and is made of beef, cubed potatoes, onions, and spices. Other items you will find frequently on Austrian menus are sauerkraut, dumplings, potato salad, and meats such as pork, chicken, and veal prepared in a variety of ways. Another favorite is *risi bisi,* which is rice and peas, spiced with onion.

The Austrians are famous for their cakes and desserts. A delicious apple strudel is served everywhere in the country. In Salzburg you may be treated to a famous Salzburg *nockerl,* for which the cook takes eggs, flour, butter, sugar (and a little imagination), and beats them into a fluffy soufflé.

Another Austrian treat is the *Sachertorte,* which was invented by Franz Sacher, a chef who worked for the great political leader, Metternich. "He kept bothering me to invent something new," Sacher once said of the famous statesman. "So I threw this together." "This" was the *Sachertorte,* a cake made with chocolate, eggs, and jam. It is often served with whipped cream or, as the Austrians say, *"mit schlag."*

Perhaps you'd like to make an Austrian cake yourself. Here is a recipe for *Kinderzwieback* (children's teacake):

2 eggs	2 tablespoons sugar
2 tablespoons flour	¼ teaspoon baking powder

Separate the egg whites from the yolks. Add the sugar to the yolks and beat them with an egg beater until they are creamy and thick. Whip the whites until they are stiff. Combine the flour and baking powder. Fold egg whites into the yolks alternately with the flour. Bake until brown at about 325 degrees in a buttered and floured cake-pan. Remove the cake from the pan while it is hot and let it cool on a rack. *Then let it stand for 24 hours.* When you are ready to eat it, cut the cake into quarter-inch slices and toast in the oven on both sides. Sprinkle with vanilla and serve.

When you have made and eaten *Kinderzwieback,* you will have come into contact with a little bit of Austria!

A boy carries hay from a high field too steep for horse and wagon.

11

Austria at Work

Because Austria is such a delightful place to visit, we sometimes forget that her recovery from poverty and ruin after terrible war damage is the result of old-fashioned hard work. Her farming, like her industry, has expanded enormously in the last fifty years. Earlier, Hungary provided Austria with much of its food, but after the Austro-Hungarian Empire broke up in 1919, Austria's seven million people had to become more self-sufficient.

AGRICULTURE AND FORESTRY

Austria's geography influences the kind of farming that goes on in each area. The mountains of western Austria are not suitable for growing grain and vegetables, and so this area is noted for cattle raising. Here the grazing land is as rich high in the mountains as it is along the lower slopes and valleys. Grass and water are plentiful. The lower meadows are not grazed by the cattle during the summer months, since the farmers let the grass grow for late mowing. Hay is stored in the little sheds that dot the lower slopes.

At the beginning of summer, the cattle are taken from their barns and led high into the mountains, an occasion which, like many others in Austria, calls for a colorful ceremony. The

Kaprun is one of Europe's largest hydroelectric power plants.

cattle are decorated with flowers and bright ribbons, and the lead cow wears a large bell around her neck. Sometimes the village priest blesses the cattle before they leave.

The upper pastures where the cattle spend the summer are called *almen*. Here they are watched over by cowherds; often the cowherds are young girls who spend the summer in these lonely places, perhaps two or three days' distance from the farms. In the fall, the cattle are brought back to their barns. The hay, cut from the lower slopes, is stored in barns and cowsheds, and it will be their feed during the long winter when the fields lie under deep snow.

As the mountains drop away, flattening out into plateaus and plains in the eastern part of Austria, the soil becomes richer. There grow the fields of grain and sugar beet. Other important Austrian crops are potatoes, cabbage, and a variety of fruits such as grapes, strawberries, cherries, and apricots. Swine are raised all over the country to satisfy the Austrians' demand for pork.

The women also work in the fields, raking hay or helping the men with their other chores. In Tyrol there is a story about a peasant girl named Notburga. She was a hard worker, but she did not like to work on Sunday which she respected as the Lord's Day. One Sunday, when she was forced to go to the fields, she tossed her sickle up into the air and asked the Lord to make it hang there as a sign that she was right. The sickle stuck on a sunbeam. Today there is a shrine in Tyrol dedicated to St. Notburga.

Much of Austria is covered by forests. Timber, therefore, is an important product and is cut even in the winter, when the lumbermen use sleds to take the logs out of the mountains. Pine, larch, beech, maple, and ash are found in mountain areas. Smaller forests of poplar, willow, and elm grow along the rivers in eastern Austria.

From wood the Austrians build houses and manufacture packing cases, toys, matches, and paper. Pressboard, made by a special process invented in Austria, is also an important

Inside a Vienna factory, these women are working on electric motors.

product. The government, which encourages conservation of the country's natural resources, has a program to plant new trees to replace those that are cut down.

INDUSTRIES AND PROFESSIONS

Austria, for a small country, has a large mining industry. Besides the iron ore, coal, oil, and the salt already mentioned, there are ore deposits of lead, zinc, and magnesite. The iron and steel industries, which were in ruins at the end of World War II, are now flourishing in Austria, as are the oil refineries and chemical factories. Electricity from Austria's large hydro-electric and steam-power plants supplies these factories. Grateful Austrians remember that it was from the United States that their nation received nearly one billion dollars in Marshall Plan aid, which permitted their industries to rebuild after World War II.

While heavy industries continue to expand in Austria, the smaller industries survive, too. There are over 150,000 small private businesses which produce everything from glass and porcelain to hand-carved toys, costume jewelry, and Christmas decorations.

One of Austria's most important industries is tourism. Long a favorite country for other European travelers, Austria is becoming popular with American tourists, too. Thousands of Austrians make their living from the hotels, restaurants, ski resorts, gift shops, and other tourist businesses.

The Austrians are truly a careful people, and most of them look forward to drawing a pension after they have retired. That is why so many Austrians wish to go into government work. The civil service is similar to the "Most High Service" that administered the empire for hundreds of years under the Habsburgs. Many of the country's outstanding opera stars and musicians are paid by the government; they are members of the civil service and receive pensions when they retire.

Austria has played an important role in the development of science and medicine. Men like Carl Auer von Welsbach, who invented the incandescent gas mantle, and Viktor Kaplan, inventor of the low-pressure Kaplan turbine, have contributed to modern science.

A Viennese doctor, Sigmund Freud, founded psychoanalysis, a method of treating people with emotional and mental disorders. Believing that many of these disorders may be traced to something that happened to them before the age of six, Freud asked his patients to try to remember in detail certain events of their early lives. He hoped that as they talked to him, the source of their trouble would come to light.

Freud came to the United States only once, to lecture at Clark University in Massachusetts. His ideas have had a great influence not only in this country but throughout the world. His work has been important to modern medicine, psychology, philosophy, literature, and art.

This craftsman is carefully hand-finishing porcelain figurines, using methods that have been employed for generations.

The Austrian Parliament building on the Ringstrasse in Vienna

12

A Democratic Republic

Austria, like the United States, is a federal republic. This means that its provinces are bound together in a federation, or league, under a republican form of government. In a republican government the supreme power rests with the citizens of the country, and they delegate this power to the representatives they vote into office.

The Austrian Constitution, which was adopted in 1920, is very much like ours. In fact, certain features of the American Constitution were used in the Austrian one. Human freedoms are guaranteed. All citizens may vote when they reach the age of twenty-one. There are two houses in Austria's parliament, just as there are two in the American Congress. Austria's lower house, the *Nationalrat* (National Council), has 165 members, who are elected by the people. Its upper house, the *Bundesrat* (Federal Council), has 50 members, who are elected by the legislators of each province. (United States senators used to be elected by the state legislatures, until the Seventeenth Amendment to the Constitution changed this in 1913.)

Every six years the Austrian people elect a new president. The president then appoints a chancellor (or prime minister), who in turn selects a group of ministers. The president is also the commander-in-chief of the Austrian Army.

Austria's democratic way of life survived the terrors of Nazism before and during World War II. Taken over by Hitler in 1938, Austria was recognized by the Allied governments (the United States, Great Britain, France, and Russia) as the Nazis' first victim nation. It was decided that at the end of the war Austria would be treated as a liberated country such as France, and not as an enemy country like Germany.

Russia broke its promise, however, and Austria had to wait almost ten years for its freedom. After the war Austria was divided into zones, occupied by the Allied armies. Russia tried to impose a communist government on its zone, just as it did in East Germany, but the Austrian people stood firm. They resisted all communist attempts to take over, and voted down almost all Communist Party candidates in the elections.

When Russia finally agreed to sign the State Treaty in 1955, it made Austria buy back the oil wells, river steamers, factories,

and other materials Russia had seized in 1945. Today Austria is bound by the terms of that treaty to remain neutral, but its sympathies clearly lie with the non-communist countries. Since many of its old markets in eastern Europe have been cut off behind the Iron Curtain, Austria is more and more dependent on the West. Today about half of its export trade is with the nations of the Common Market (Italy, France, West Germany, Belgium, the Netherlands, and Luxembourg). The rest of its trade is with other nations of the free world.

TYROL PROBLEM

The international problem which most affects the Austrian people today is the dispute over South Tyrol. Tourists visiting Innsbruck will see dramatic evidence of the inhabitants' feelings, for whitewashed everywhere on rocks and buildings are block-lettered slogans which demand "Freedom for South Tyrol." This problem was created when the lower half of Tyrol and its German-speaking population were taken from Austria and given to Italy to govern after World War I.

Italy had claimed for many years that its natural boundary was the Brenner Pass. But the pass was located in what was formerly the center of Tyrol. In existence for over a thousand years, Tyrol was first an independent mountain state and later an Austrian province. Before World War I only three per cent of South Tyrol's population was Italian.

The Allies gave in to Italian demands in 1919 because that country had been one of them. Later Woodrow Wilson, President of the United States at that time, admitted that to divide Tyrol had been "a serious mistake." Between wars the Italian dictator Mussolini tried to make South Tyrol "Italian." He prohibited the speaking of German in official places and brought in thousands of workers from the south of Italy. Yet today, two-thirds of the area's people speak German.

Again, after World War II, these people looked to the Allies for help. Despite the English Prime Minister Winston Churchill's opinion that South Tyrol should be returned to Austria, the Allies left it in Italian hands.

The Allies' viewpoint was this: Austria had been the center of the Austro-Hungarian Empire in World War I, and so was treated as an enemy. During World War II some of its leaders and people had sided with Germany. Austria was thought not altogether blameless by many of the Allied leaders.

Italy then signed an agreement with Austria, promising justice for the South Tyrolese. Today Austria claims that Italy has not lived up to that agreement. She charges that the Italians still use many of Mussolini's policies in their attempt to destroy the language and culture of South Tyrol. Instead of giving South Tyrol a certain amount of freedom (or a voice in governing itself) as promised, Italy simply joined it to a larger Italian province. The South Tyrolese are therefore outvoted in the elections and have no real autonomy, no separate government. Many Austrians have friends and relatives in South Tyrol, and they hope to see the argument settled by the United Nations.

FRIENDSHIP WITH AMERICA

Austrians, for the most part, are very friendly to Americans. There is, in fact, an Austrian-American Society which has branches in several Austrian cities. The branch in Innsbruck is especially active. Set at the far end of a lovely garden, the society's building there is more than just a reading room where visiting Americans may rest their feet and thumb through the latest magazines from home. It brings together many Austrians whose only common bond seems to be an interest in America.

"For many years we Austrians were closed in from the outside world by the Nazis," a society member will say. "When World War II ended we were curious to find out what other people were doing. America has always interested us. So a group of Austrians founded this society."

Students gather outside a modern Hauptschule in a Vienna suburb.

The society started chapters in Austria's biggest cities and worked closely with the "America Houses" set up by the United States Information Service (USIS) immediately after the war. When the USIS closed its America House in Innsbruck it turned over its building and its library to the Austrian-American Society. Today the society has over two thousand members.

In the late afternoon the library may house a class of Austrian schoolchildren, chanting their English phrases in loud voices. The children pay forty cents a month for English lessons, while the adults pay a little more. American cultural films are shown; lectures are given by visiting American professors. In the evening the building may be taken over by youth groups who play the society's collection of jazz records.

YOUTH AND EDUCATION

The Austrian people take their education seriously. Austria claims the lowest rate of illiteracy in the world; less than two per cent of its people cannot read or write. All Austrian children must go to school for at least nine years. While boys and girls usually go to separate schools, there are some schools where they attend classes together.

Many Austrian children go to kindergarten before beginning their regular schooling. Kindergarten, in fact, is a German word, meaning "children's garden." All children must start school at the age of six. In some small villages the elementary school contains the first eight grades, often all in the same room and all taught by the same teacher, as in the "little red school-houses" of early America.

In most cases Austrian elementary schools, called *Volks-schulen* (people's schools), contain only the first four grades. Children go to school at about eight o'clock in the morning and continue until one o'clock in the afternoon. They study history, arithmetic, geography, religion, and, of course, the German language. There are short recesses between classes; during one of them the children are served free milk.

At the end of four years the children are ready to go on to "secondary schools." One group goes to the *Hauptschulen*, which contains four more grades and gives the child a sound general education, preparing him to go right to work. The other group goes to the *Mittelschulen*, which is an eight-year course and prepares the student for colleges and universities. Here he is taught science, languages, music, art, and physical education. Girls also take courses in home economics and child care. Almost all Austrian children study English for at least five years.

The student who graduates from *Mittelschulen* has completed twelve years of school (just like our high-school graduate) and is ready for college. Austria has a number of colleges and universities, including the University of Vienna (founded 1365), the University of Graz (founded 1585), and the University of Innsbruck (founded 1677). There is also the Military Academy at Wiener Neustadt, which is the Austrian West Point.

Austria takes great care in preparing her young people for the responsibilities they must some day share in managing their country. No human talent is wasted. If a child has started out in the *Hauptschulen* and shows the kind of ability which might be put to better advantage in a university, he is allowed to transfer to the *Mittelschulen* and prepare for a university education. Handicapped children, too, are trained especially so that they may take their place in society.

Perhaps there is no better example of Austria's care for her young people than the new program which is becoming famous all over the world, the S.O.S. This program was started after World War II by a man from Vorarlberg named Hermann Gmeiner. Mr. Gmeiner decided to do something about Austria's orphaned and unwanted children.

Girls in a cooking class in an Austrian Mittelschule

His plan was simple. He believed that a young child needs a mother's love and the security he can find only in family life. An orphan who is placed in an orphanage is not likely to get the attention he needs, and so he will always feel himself to be an outsider.

In 1948 Hermann Gmeiner founded his first S.O.S. Children's Village at Imst in Tyrol. It was set up so that each child would be raised in a "family" setting. Eight or nine children were assigned to each clean, pleasant house, along with a "mother." This mother was an unmarried woman or a widow who devoted all of her time to these children. She remained with them until they were grown. She gave them the love and devotion they would have received if they had had mothers of their own.

The children in each house became "brothers and sisters" to each other. The older children looked after the younger ones. In many cases there were actually brothers and sisters living in one house, for four and five members (in one case there were *nine* members) of a family came there together. These children lived just as they would have in a real home. The "mother" did all the cooking for them. They celebrated holidays together. They went to the school in Imst along with all the other children from "real" homes.

The S.O.S. Children's Village at Imst was so successful that soon others were started in different parts of Austria. Then they spread to other European countries. People who did not have S.O.S. Villages in their areas sent contributions to help pay the cost of running them in distant lands. Americans have been especially generous in sending money to S.O.S. Hermann Gmeiner hopes someday to start an S.O.S. Children's Village in the United States.

Meanwhile, today's young Austrians are growing up to treasure the glories of their country's past and the opportunities in their new democracy. They are their country's hope for even brighter accomplishments in the Austria of tomorrow.

An S.O.S. Children's Village and one of its "families"

For Further Reading

BOOKS

Baedeker, Karl. *Baedeker's Autoguide: Austria*. New York: Macmillan Company, 1959.

Baedeker, Karl. *Tyrol and Salzburg*. New York: The Macmillan Company, 1961.

Czernin, Count Ferdinand. *This Salzburg*. Vienna: Frick, 1937.

Esterhazy, Christa. *The Young Traveller in Austria*. Newton Centre, Mass.: Branford, 1956.

Gibbon, Monk. *Austria*. New York: W. W. Norton & Company, 1962.

Graf-Khittel, Gita. *Austria, Music and Theatre*. Trans. by Oscar Konstandt. Innsbruck: Pinguin-Verlag, 1958.

Hiscocks, Richard. *The Rebirth of Austria*. London and New York: Oxford University Press, 1953.

Kohn, Hans. *Habsburg Empire, 1804–1918*. Princeton: Van Nostrand Press, 1961.

May, Arthur J. *The Habsburg Monarchy, 1867–1914*. Cambridge: Harvard University Press, 1951.

Nawrath, Dr. Alfred, and others. *Austria: 160 Photographs*. London: Studio, 1956.

Reynolds, James. *Panorama of Austria*. New York: G. P. Putnam's Sons, 1956.

Shepherd, Gordon. *The Austrian Odyssey*. New York: St. Martin's Press, 1957.

Vausson, Claude. *Austria*. New York: The Viking Press, 1960.

Wechsberg, Joseph. *Avalanche!* New York: Alfred A. Knopf, 1958.

Wohlrabe, Raymond A. *The Land and People of Austria*. Philadelphia: J. B. Lippincott Company, 1956.

ARTICLES

Bemelmans, L. "Soul of Austria," *Holiday* (August, 1962).

Bowie, B. M. "Building a New Austria," *National Geographic Magazine* (February, 1959).

Gallico, P. "Silent Night; Birthplace of Christmastide's Best-loved Carol," *Saturday Evening Post* (December 15, 1962).

Hauser, E. O. "Our Neutral Friends the Austrians," *Saturday Evening Post* (June 8, 1957).

Morton, F. "Innsbruck," *Holiday* (January, 1961).

Morton, F. "Tyrol," *Holiday* (January, 1960).

Wechsberg, J. "Vienna's Festival Marathon," *Saturday Review* (July 14, 1962).

Index